BETWEEN FURY
AND PEACE

The Many Arts of Derek Walcott

ARROWSMITH

PRESS

Between Fury and Peace
The Many Arts of Derek Walcott

© 2022 Arrowsmith Press
All Rights Reserved

ISBN: 978-1-7376156-9-9

Boston — New York — San Francisco — Baghdad
San Juan — Kyiv — Istanbul — Santiago, Chile
Beijing — Paris — London — Cairo — Madrid
Milan — Melbourne — Jerusalem — Darfur

11 Chestnut St.
Medford, MA 02155

arrowsmithpress@gmail.com
www.arrowsmithpress.com

The Forty-Sixth Arrowsmith book
was typeset & designed by Ezra Fox
for Askold Melnyczuk & Alex Johnson
in Palatino and Palatino Linotype fonts

Derek Walcott published material reprinted
by permission of Farrar, Straus and Giroux.

Derek Walcott unpublished material printed by permission
of Farrar, Straus and Giroux on behalf of the Walcott Estate.

Front Cover Image: *At the gate, Petit Valley*, c. 1981, Derek Walcott
Watercolour on paper

Back Cover Sketch by Van Howell, courtesy of Eva Salzman

BETWEEN FURY AND PEACE

The Many Arts of Derek Walcott

Edited by Askold Melnyczuk

CONTENTS

INTRODUCTION

BETWEEN FURY AND PEACE:
DEREK WALCOTT'S VISIONARY GLEAM

Askold Melnyczuk

Back in 1982, word on the street was that the best conversation in Boston was to be had at 236 Bay State Road Monday mornings at 9 a.m.

9 a.m.? Mondays? Seriously? Recently returned to town after several years of productive drift, I decided to check it out.

The conversation turned out to be a monologue, thank God, and I don't overstate when I say that not only were the rumors true, but that sitting in on Derek Walcott's classes as an interloper those many Mondays changed my life.

In a voice that echoed with the gravel of a rising tide, brimming with a coiled energy that unfurled as he spoke, Walcott talked to us about Dante and Auden, Graves and

Frank O'Hara, Poussin and Eddie Murphy. He was in dialogue with all of them. The world's great poets were his posse, his contemporaries. He paid them respect by memorizing their poems, about which he spoke as an insider, as though he'd written them himself. An hour might pass parsing a line of Keats': "The hare limped, trembling, through the frozen grass." Negative capability let the poet view the world from the perspective of the hounded hare: can't you see, don't you feel, the shiver inside the caesura, the trembling between the commas, themselves blades of frozen grass? Here was language as mimesis, the recognition of the intimate connection between words and things. Derek showed us that words at the nano level offered a portal into other dimensions, transcending time.

Time was an ocean of endless tears, he wrote in a lyric for the Broadway musical *Capeman*, and memory was always his moving target. Derek said more than once that what he wanted was neither fame nor glory (anyway, them he had) but continuance, by which he meant (or so I understood it) he wanted to write lines that would root in readers' memories the way so many stanzas by Auden, Hardy, Edward Thomas and, to everyone's surprise, Walter de la Mare, had stuck with him.

He was a brilliant mimic who loved puns and politically heinous jokes which he told, eyes burning, with a wicked mirth. A glamor trailed in his wake. That shabby room on Bay State Road echoed with the names of his friends and collaborators—Baryshnikov, Arthur Miller, Toni Morrison. Friendships mattered to Walcott. More than one of his pals swaggered in or came to lunch at Chef Chang's or dropped by the theater, or the Walcott apartment on St. Mary's Street. I recall a hungover Thom Gunn, a fast-talking James Fenton, a Nobel laureate named Brodsky lying on the floor, blowing smoke rings and complaining about his reviews. One evening I shuffled out of a performance by Derek's Trinidad Theatre Workshop alongside Paul Simon.

Ever generous with both what and whom he knew, as well as with the tangible bounty the world bestowed on him, Derek took us out to lunch, paid for dinner for a dozen, and even invited a few of us to join him for breakfast which, given that he rose before dawn, came a little late for him, a little early for us.

His famous discipline was simultaneously daunting and inspiring. I remember dropping by one morning at eight—he had already done his writing for the day and was working on a painting, the easel set up in his modest study.

Flaubert, lamenting his own word-squeezing ways, envied the prodigality of Victor Hugo, whom he described as prolific as nature itself, and I remember Seamus Heaney asking Derek to account for his own "obscene fecundity." I wish I remembered the answer.

In the end, though, we sought out Walcott's company not to touch the hem or for the free lunch or to meet his celebrated friends. What brought us together was Derek's music. Walcott's first full-length book, *In a Green Night*, came wrapped in a green band on which was printed Robert Graves' unqualified endorsement: "Derek Walcott handles English with a closer understanding of its inner magic than most (if not any) of his English contemporaries."

Music wasn't the whole of it, though. Extemporizing about Wallace Stevens, Walcott once quipped that the insurance executive's poems made him want to cry out "Nice noise, Wally!" Derek took seriously his own frequently repeated claim that a poet's proper companions were historians and philosophers. He used his verse very much as had his beloved Wystan, as a vehicle of thought. His poems' passionate engagement with the complexities of history enact a mind attempting to think and feel its way to a place of freedom. From the start his poetry probed neocolonial narratives, deriding empire's assumptions and scorning its self-regard and privileges. Big questions—about identity, about one's place in history—resonated from the start in poems such as "A Far Cry From Africa" in which he interrogates the self-division that's familiar to anyone with a bifurcated identity:

> Where shall I turn, divided to the vein?
> I who have cursed
> The drunken officer of British rule, how choose
> Between this Africa and the English tongue I love?
> Betray them both, or give back what they give?
> How can I face such slaughter and be cool?
> How can I turn from Africa and live?

His understanding of what it meant to live in the shadow of empire doubtless made him more receptive than most to the Ukrainian story I was struggling to write, unsure of what to do with it, how to tell it. He actively encouraged confronting its complexities. He even showed an early version of my first novel to his publisher. He might sometimes have regretted this gift of his trust. When he handed me a typescript of an early version of *Omeros* he surely wasn't expecting that I'd have the hubris to call and offer a line-by-line critique of the epic for which he'd soon receive his Nobel. I remember pausing after a series of suggestions about how he might tighten a stanza and, noting the deep silence on the other end, asking "Is this too much, Derek?" "Getting there," he said with a laugh.

I am writing this as Russian forces continue savaging Ukrainian cities in yet another attempt to wipe the country off the map. Mass graves have been found in Bucha and sighted around Mariupol where the number of dead may climb into the tens of thousands. Russia's genocidal assault forces the question: what matters? Of what use can poetry be at such a time? "The classics can console/but not enough," Walcott wrote in *Sea Grapes*.

Not enough, perhaps, and yet in moments of extreme intensity the balm offered by the right words in the right order can surprise. One step beyond the meliorating power of music and philosophical reflection is that rarest mode of verse which is able to turn readers into witnesses to, and participants in, what I'll call the "visionary gleam." More than a reminder of our capacity for transcendence, such poems are capable of enfolding, however briefly, its readers into their own articulated ecstasy. This rarest of qualities may be found in Donne, Wordsworth, Blake, Hopkins, Yeats, Dickinson, Whitman.

The visionary gleam, voiced in a tone of breathtaking tenderness, sounded early in Walcott's work. There's a remarkable passage in the autobiographical, book-length early poem, *Another Life*:

About the August of my fourteenth year
I lost my self somewhere above a valley…
Afternoon light ripened the valley,
rifling smoke climbed from small labourers' houses,
and I dissolved into a trance.
I was seized by a pity more profound
than my young body could bear, I climbed
with the labouring smoke,
I drowned in labouring breakers of bright cloud,
then uncontrollably I began to weep,
inwardly, without tears, with a serene extinction
of all sense; I felt compelled to kneel…

As the poet's self dissolves into his surroundings, he's overwhelmed with pity: "I wept for nothing and for everything, / I wept for the earth of the hill under my knees, / for the grass, the pebbles, for the cooking smoke / above the labourers' houses...." Part of what startles me about the passage is how much it reminds me of one of the seminal pieces by the 19th century Ukrainian poet, Taras Shevchenko who wrote, "I was nearing the end of my thirteenth year, / shepherding a flock of lambs above the village / when suddenly I felt irradiated by a tenderness / that seemed to fall from heaven...."

Poetry's visionary mode may well be the hardest to pull off in our secular age. When it succeeds it does more than remind us of the multiple dimensions of being. Such poetry is nothing less than a transcript of extraordinary perceptions accessible to all, always, even amid the most ordinary and mundane of circumstances, as well as at life's most difficult moments. "The Season of Phantasmal Peace" brings together Walcott's heightened responsiveness to the conciliatory powers of the natural world, in a lyric of nearly supernatural sympathy and insight: "Then all the nations of birds lifted together / the huge net of the shadows of this earth...." The poet elaborates this extraordinary image in which flocks of birds passing above a city somehow pull away whatever darkness lies between us and a radical reality: "until / there was no longer dusk, or season, decline, or weather, / only this passage of phantasmal light / that not the narrowest shadow dared to sever."

The poem goes on to describe the incomprehension of the city's inhabitants as the light floods in—they see the birds but don't understand what's happening. These are not ornamental or generic birds. Because the poet knows the powers of the particular, and the mystery inherent in proper nouns, he names them: ospreys, killdeer, the ember-circling chough. The poet then ascribes a sublime intentionality to the birds, who "from the high privilege of their birth" are capable of feeling "something brighter than pity for the wingless ones/below them who shared dark holes in windows and in houses." And so the birds continue peeling back the darkness "above all change, betrayals of falling suns,/and this season lasted one moment, like the pause/ between dusk and darkness, between fury and peace,/but for such as our earth is now, it lasted long."

Indeed.

Essays

DEREK WALCOTT:
"THE ARKANSAS TESTAMENT"

Peter Balakian

I first met Derek Walcott in May 1985 when my friend
Michael Harper brought him to Colgate for a reading. I had
brought Michael to Colgate for the semester as a visiting
poet, and Michael and Derek had been friends for a long
time. That evening in Brehmer Theater Michael gave one
of his imaginative, meandering, full of love introductions
to Derek. Derek came on stage, said nothing, and as I
would learn, this was his style. He simply announced the
title of each poem before he read it. If you hadn't heard
Walcott read, which I hadn't, I would be surprised if you
weren't as riveted by his mode of reading as I was. The
voice: his cadence, phrasing, tonal gravitas. The music
of his eloquent Caribbean English. I had never heard
anything like it. I still haven't. I was locked in, sitting

there in the dark of the theater.

He said very little between poems. He didn't believe in the poetry reading as an occasion for story telling or reminiscing. Occasionally he would give bits of context for a poem. Most of the time, he just announced each title: "This is called "Light of the World," this is "God Rest Ye Merry Gentlemen, Part II," or this one is called "The Arkansas Testament," which would be the title of his next book. When the book came out in 1987 I saw that he was reading, that evening, an earlier version of the poem. After the reading we went to the Colgate Inn for the nightcap moment. Derek ordered a burger and a Coke.

"The Arkansas Testament" is a poem of introspection and historical and moral witness in which Walcott weaves probes of his own soul with a vision of racism in America. The poem encounters a black man who is spending a night in a motel in the American South of Little Rock, Arkansas, and its structure is both expansive and formal—with its twenty-four sections of sixteen lines that move between iambic trimeter and tetrameter, often with subtle ABAB rhymes. The culture of racism and the history of slavery are ubiquitous in fact and imagination as the poem opens with an elaborate conceit of a Confederate soldiers' graveyard "Over Fayettville, Arkansas, / a slope of memorial pines / guards the stone slabs of forces / fallen for the Confederacy / at some point in the Civil War." In a poem that is shaped by light, Walcott arrives at his motel as midwinter "dusk," and a "surrendering sun" lead him along Highway 71 to the "brass numbered doors / of my $17.50 motel," where he is "Jet-lagged and gritty." In this Walcottian poem of extravagant metaphor, the poet falls into his "double bed / like Saul under neighing horses / on the highway to Damascus." The unconverted Saul—a metaphor for the poet's sense of his own fallen self.

Then we get the motel room with its "Celotex ceiling, TV, telephone," "parking lot through cinder blocks," in this entrapped space inside the "chained door" he feels "homesick for islands with fringed shores." At the front desk where he goes to pay for his room, his biting wit and clipped dialogue remind us that he is also a great playwright: "How'll you pay for this, sir? Cash or change?" "I missed the chance of answering , 'In kind,' like my colour." In what becomes a strange monastic-like chamber of a cheap motel room where the bare walls flash a neon sign reflection, and there is "no lamp," "no magazine," "no shelves," just the smell of "detergent pine," and "a smudge of the wall"—Walcott finds the setting for his interrogation. In section VI he confesses—and this poem is a confession—that being "unshaven" and "unshowered" is a trope for being "unsaved," and reeking "of the natural coward/I am." The poem slides seamlessly from self-reckoning to the poet's collective sense of self as a Black man; he conflates this "place for/ disposable shavers," with a place for "my own disposable people!"

When he wakes from his "dead drunk" sleep, the streets of Fayetteville Arkansas overwhelm him with the ironies of the landscape with its "white-neon crucifix," "sweet smell" of a "barn door opening," and "Confederate gray" sky. As he heads out at 5 AM to the local diner for his "caffeine fix," his omnivorous metaphor-making mind sees the legacy of Jim Crow apartheid everywhere: the "revolving red eye on top/of a cruising police car" and in "all-night garage," "the gums of a toothless sybil/in garage tires, and she said: "STAY BLACK AND INVISIBLE/TO THE SIRENS OF ARKANSAS." He's reminded that his "shadow still hurts the South/like "Lee's slowly reversing sword."

As the poet walks into the day, the poem becomes a morning-time walpurgisnacht—where the evil spirits of the past, slavery and apartheid— imbue the present. In Section XII, the demons are everywhere. Passing "a cafeteria" to get his morning coffee, he sees the predicament of "his race,": "a tall black cook," and a "beehive-blonde waitress," some white guys with "Deere caps," and just sound of the "muttering black decanter" evokes "Sherman's smoking march to Atlanta / or the march to Montgomery." He "bags" the "hot Styrofoam coffee," as the stream of associations pour— reminding him of the "recently repealed law that any black person out after curfew could be shot dead in Arkansas." Morning sunlight is "Aryan light," evoking South African apartheid—"the seam glints in the mind" to the "golden white supremacy of "Witwatersrand," and "Boer's sunburnt hand." Across the globe, white supremacy is something "in their blood."

In Section XV, walking through this "average mid-American town" in the "cold sunshine," the poet feels his age in the "nips of arthritis," and it is in the ordinariness of middle America—"brown motels, burger haciendas" in this "neat evangelical town," of "God fearing folks," that the evil of racism is still so alive, and again Walcott sees the shadows of the Civil War in the landscape of pine scented air— "gray divisions [of the Confederacy] and dates." The landscape is imbued for him with visions of history: "Perhaps in these same pines runs / with cross ties of bleeding thorns, / the track of the Underground Rail- / road way up into Canada." "the tinkle of ankle chains / running north, where history is harder / to bear: the hypocrisy / of clouds with Puritan collars......" "wounds from the Indian Wars.... / leaves tumble like Hessians" "churches / arrow into the Shawmut sky." Landscapes of granular reality and historical allegory merge in Walcott's baroque flourishes of sunlight. Nature is stained by history—everywhere—human evil invading the organic. No Emersonian sublime in this poem, though

Walcott would often find that sublime in his Caribbean landscapes. As he embraces his Black invisibility, here his shadow's "scribbled question" asks: "Will I be a citizen/ or an afterthought of the state?"

In Section XX, Walcott engages some big questions: how can he—"sing"— write his poems—in the face of the American flag that has been blotted out by "the ghosts/ of sheeted hunters who ride/to the fire-white cross of the South." In the conundrum of the poet's relationship to the nation (in this case Walcott's adopted nation), he asks: can I "share my art," "pretend that it is all past and curse/from the picket lines of my verse/the concept of Apartheid?" Walcott closes Section XX with a pithy truism: "What we know of evil/is that it will never end." In the penultimate moment of the poem—meted out as it is in iambic tetrameter—the scalding "sin" of racism stalks him as he moves along the street and sees the naked vulnerability of black men who cower in the gaze of the "hooded eyes of a cop," (an image with many contemporary associations). Walcott's feels it all as "acid in the gut," the "poison infecting the hill pines/ all the way to the top."

In the final sections he comes full circle to his monastic motel room to address his maker:

> Sir, you urge us to divest
> ourselves of all earthly things
> like these camphor cabinets
> with their fake pine coffins;
> to empty the drawer of the chest
> and look far beyond the hurt
> on which a cross looks down
> as light floods the asphalt

In a poem that confronts limitations—human evil, the self, mortality, he also faces the limitations of his art—acknowledging that " there are things that my craft cannot wield,/and one is power," which leads him to think of two great poets —Sir Walter Raleigh and Francois Villon—facing their executions "cowering in the shadow of the still knot"— one vision of memento mori.

From this banal motel room in middle America— he confesses:

> this, Sir, is my Office,
> my Arkansas Testament,
> my two cupfuls of Cowardice,
> my sure, unshaven Salvation,
> my people predicament,

The poignant tension between personal failure and America's crippling racism keeps this motel room drama in paradoxical perspective. The sacramental rhetoric of the poem embodies self-acceptance, as the quotidian unspools with the psychological: "Bless the increasing bliss/of truck tires over asphalt,/and these stains I cannot remove/from the self-soiled heart."

The trope of impressionistic light continues to shade and illuminate as the sun on the flag transforms the room: "afternoon sun will reprint/the bars of a flag whose cloth—/must heal the stripes and scars." The poem ends with the poet's visionary seeing, as the light emanating from the TV he's just turned on, flashes in his mind with an expanse of America, and Walcott's painterly imagination renders what he calls "amber successive stills" in a rush of light: from the "waves off Narragansett" to the "gold bars" of light on the "wagon axles of Mormons" to the

"Black Hills," the "Mojave," "Vegas, "the pipe organs of the Sequoias," and to the "Pacific," before 'The Today Show,' comes on the screen. The irony of the banal morning TV show closing the poet's agonized, private journey, reminds me of the way Eliot has "human voices" wake Prufrock at the end of his journey to the interior self in "The Love Song of J. Alfred Prufrock," so that "we drown" back into the cauterizing world of daily events. Walcott's visit to a cheap motel room of Deep South, middle America, in the cold sun of mid-winter is a journey into self and history in an intertwining way that embodies several veins of Walcott's sensibility and astonishing linguistic resources.

Years later when Derek and Sigrid invited me and Helen and our children Sophia and James to spend a week with them on Saint Lucia for a mid-winter holiday escape from freezing, snow covered central New York, I experienced that Caribbean light that had nurtured Derek's life and imagination. The sun on hibiscus, frangipani, and green palms. The morning light on the calm turquoise sea, or the noon light on a man in a boat just off shore blowing through a conch shell. I spent a couple afternoons in Derek's painting studio looking at the watercolors he was working on. He was a good painter of watercolors—he loved light and water, light on rocks, light on clouds, light on big green fronds of plants whose names I didn't know. Standing in his studio, I thought of "The Arkansas Testament," and how even in darkness, Derek made astonishing swaths of light to see more deeply the complexities and contradictions of human experience.

DEREK WALCOTT'S
UPSTATE GHOST DANCE

Robert Bensen

Derek Walcott was the first writer I wanted to bring to Hartwick College, when the shiny new assistant professor I was arrived in 1978. Few of the next 39 years would pass without him visiting the college, often more than once a year. He read from every new book from *The Star-Apple Kingdom* (1979) to *White Egrets* (2010), visited classes, and conducted writing and acting workshops. He wrote a full-length play, *The Ghost Dance* (1989), for the Hartwick theatre students to perform. Sometimes he brought Joseph Brodsky to read with him. In St. Lucia and Trinidad, he hosted my off-campus classes in West Indian literature. Every year a larger circle of friends and devotees enjoyed his company. For nearly four decades, this small college in the Catskills was richly blessed by a great poet and playwright.

I like to think he and his work benefited as well, beginning with "Upstate," a poem he wrote after his first visit in April 1979. Having read to the college audience "The Schooner *Flight*" from *The Star-Apple Kingdom*, he returned to New York City on the Trailways bus. On the ride through the Catskills' "repetitive" villages, the poet allows this new but worn landscape to invade, then transform him. He begins in winter-worn melancholy but discovers a spring-borne desire in the "sun-freckled" hills to become part of this landscape by learning "to speak like birch or aspen confidently." His is not a romance of calendar images, but a growing sympathy with the land and those who live there.

Walcott transforms the commonplace trope of trees uttering leaves as a form of speech to find means to instill, into his poetry, an indigenous sensibility. Perhaps he had in mind the "talking leaves" that Sequoya observed white men reading, which moved him to invent the Cherokee syllabary. "Upstate" might be said to contain the seed of *The Ghost Dance*, revealing a way to move beyond the literature of extinction, as in his treatment of Kalinago genocide in "The Schooner *Flight*," wherein Shabine dreams he is a Kalinago, falling and perishing in Dominica (alluding to legends about Kalinagos who leapt to their deaths in Grenada, Martinique, and Dominica). In "Upstate," he is determined to learn a new way of speaking by putting "the cold small pebbles from the spring / upon my tongue" and speak "like birch or aspen confidently." The lines may be Whitmanesque ("Clear images! Direct as your daughters / in the way their clear look returns your stare…"), but Whitman's verse incorporates his admiration for Native speech as fitting the American landscape, and he aimed to "pronounce what the air holds of the red aborigines," in *Leaves of Grass*.

Derek especially liked coming Upstate in October. He enjoyed getting out of the city and taking in fall's peak color of the hardwood forests but was hardly the average fall-foliage tourist. For him, the season's beauty bore reminders of the region's colonial history, especially the displacement of Native peoples, much as the beauty of the Antilles did not absolve the history of bondage and oppression. Being in Iroquoian lands made an Indian presence visceral for him. "There," he wrote in *Omeros* (1990, XLI), "Iroquois flashed in the Indian red, in the sepias / and ochres of leaf-mulch." In "Old New England," he wrote of railroad lines "arrowing" west to New York's "mountainwide absence of the Iroquois," of Indian trails that "trickle" down the hillside.

These primal images of this region's landscape, combined in his imagination with the still-powerful (even if discredited) myth of the "vanishing Indian," fueled his treatment of Native history in *The Ghost Dance* and *Omeros* (1990) in corresponding episodes surrounding the 1890 Wounded Knee Massacre and death of Sitting Bull. Both the play and the epic's Lakota episode center on Catherine Weldon, a white woman who was secretary and friend to Sitting Bull. Weldon gave Derek "great clarity of focus," as the play's director Duncan Smith said. Like the Lakota characters, including Kicking Horse, she was "also marginalized, powerless to stop the tragedy, just another figure in the dance of ghosts." In October 1989, a month before the play premiered, Derek was doing rewrites. He'd made himself at home on the couch, working in his meticulous, watercolorist's script. He moved to the dining room table and began typing on my Hermes manual. I spied over his shoulder to see what scene he was typing, but instead he clattered along the triple-furrowed stanzas of *Omeros*. I felt Catherine Weldon move between the play and the poem and back.

The play had its genesis in improv workshops that Derek conducted for the theatre students beginning in 1981. He returned year to year in January with bits of dialogue and scenes. But not until 1985 or 1986 did the idea for a play start to cohere. Students in Duncan Smith's reader's theatre class were building a piece around a confrontation between Minnesota farmers and some young Lakota men that led to the Dakota War of 1862. According to Director of Theatre Smith, Derek said little, but came back the next day with two Catherine Weldon scenes that would open the play. Duncan (who directed the production and played Dr. Beddoes) gave Derek a copy of *The Moon of Popping Trees* by Rex Alan Smith. That classic portrayal of the 1890 massacre at Wounded Knee and subsequent death of Sitting Bull profoundly shaped the development of the script, which plays out Catherine Weldon's role in attempting to keep peace between the Indian agent Major James McLaughlin and the Lakota warrior Kicking Bear and of course Sitting Bull—a role doomed to failure.

The Indigenous past of this region was a presence for Derek. In May 1990, we were walking down from the top of the college's hill overlooking the city of Oneonta. He paused to admire the panorama (or so I thought) of the Susquehanna Valley to the east, and the larger Catskills looming 30 miles away. We both scanned the rooftops below, the wisps of smoke from the chimneys of those habitations and businesses across the city and edging up the hillsides.

After several minutes of silence, he spoke: "Is this really better?"

I gave his question the respect of silence too, then said I didn't know. I asked what he meant. Nettled, he repeated, "Is this really better?"

I knew what he meant, all right, but I had no answer. Yes, and I'd be a colonizer. No, and I'd be a hypocrite. I told him he was asking the wrong person.

His vision of Iroquois in the painterly palette of red, sepia and ochre leaves in *Omeros* (XLI) opened to his self-reflection on human relation to place and adaptability, that "The widening mind can acquire / the hues of a foliage different from where it begins." Yet, reversing the idea ten lines later, he averred that people "take their colours / as the trees do from the native soil of their birth," so that removed from their origins, "a desert place / widens in the heart." The mind widened or the heart a desert, the ambivalence of home *versus* exile enlivens his poetry's verbal surfaces and opens its emotional depths to the displacement and dispossession of Native peoples by decades of Walcott's visiting Iroquoian land Upstate. He made the vivid colors of dying leaves an emblem of history that he explored in *The Ghost Dance* and *Omeros*. In the play, Kicking Bear says, "It is autumn now. As it is with those leaves, / so it will be with all the Indian nations […] when all the red tribes are blown across the earth, / and their leaves will be buried in your whiteness." And in *Omeros*: "Flare fast and fall, Indian flags of October! / […] redden the sumac from Maine / to the Finger Lakes" (XLI.iii).

The Ghost Dance opened November 1989 at Hartwick's Slade Theatre. The play advanced in the American College Theater Festival competition and was chosen to be given again at The Kennedy Center in January 1990. The poster for the play featured a painting by Hartwick art professor Phil Young (Cherokee/Scots-Irish), from his "Rock Shelter Spirits" series, which Derek approved with enthusiasm, surely because the central image hovers between the spirit world and this physical world, the realm of the ghost dance itself.

Recognizing Derek's contributions to Hartwick College's writing and theatre programs, President Philip

Wilder invited him to receive an honorary doctorate at the May 1990 graduation. After President Wilder made the presentation, Derek was to address the audience. He moved to the lectern and placed his papers in front of him. He began "The Season of Phantasmal Peace," in a voice that drew all to it, coming from a deep stillness unheard before on this hill. Then that voice grew relentlessly from the inaugural lines, "Then all the nations of birds lifted together / the huge net of the shadows of this earth..." and with incremental steps it enlarged toward omniscience, bearing witness to the "soundless" bird-nations in "phantasmal light" as evening drew on to night. The birds lifted the net "above all change, betrayals of falling suns" for a momentary season, "like the pause / between dusk and darkness, between fury and peace, / but, for such as our earth is now, it lasted long."

The microphone may have picked up a shuffle of papers as Walcott lifted them from the podium, or as he closed the soft pages of *The Fortunate Traveller*. But no sound touched the spell that the poem had cast over the audience. When they began to realize it had ended, applause began— scattered at first, but it spread quickly, swelling over the crowd. Two or three years later, a colleague told me she had heard Derek that day. Ever since, she wished that could happen every commencement. *If only it could*, I agreed.

If only, indeed. Derek visited less often after "The Prize" (as he called it) multiplied demands on his time. Still, he came as soon after as he could. In April 1993, more than 400 people heard him read his choice for the event, the Catherine Weldon sections of *Omeros*. He did so in honor of the *The Ghost Dance* we had performed four years before, when Weldon and Kicking Bear, who was instrumental in bringing the ghost dance to the Lakota, relived the tragedy of *The Ghost Dance* night after night. Then, audiences heard

Weldon's leave-taking of "those whom the land that gave them life belonged to— / Sitting Bull, Kicking Bear, and the leaves of the tribes." Here, as in the first poem he wrote of this region, "Upstate," he carries forward the theme of the land as the source of indigenous life expressed as a tree issues leaves, but with the burden of witnessing the tribes' destruction. In the 1993 reading from *Omeros*, Weldon spoke again through Derek Walcott. She realizes "This was history. I had no power to change it." That inevitability comes from the defeat of her hopes in the play to make peace, which she could play out by remaining aloof from the adversaries. At the end of her appearance in *Omeros*, it is as if she finally accepts Kicking Bear's demand from the beginning of *The Ghost Dance*, to "suffer with us, / … share in a famine to join all the ghosts." As an old woman in Boston at last, she sits in her parlor, starving. She has joined the suffering and famine. All along, she concludes, she had been "a leaf in the whirlwind of the Ordained." A leaf, yes. But a talking leaf.

JEAN RHYS

Sven Birkerts

I first read Derek Walcott's "Jean Rhys" in the *New Yorker*, seeking it out after Joseph Brodsky in some context announced "there is no better poem, period"—or words to that effect. Brodsky made such assertions all the time, and he was always right, at least in that glowing moment of encounter.

The poem was like some vivid dream filmed all in sepia—it struck me then, and it continues to strike me now. At the time I hadn't read the writer Jean Rhys, barely knew of her, but while she was the eponymous subject, 1 was moved by the tableau itself, which seemed to scarcely need her. Though of course it did, as I've come to see over time—and after reading her work.

I don't know if I can think of a more consistently visual or deeply atmospheric poem. It is, at once, a photograph, a text about—among other things—writing; and it is in every line a confirmation of what I think of as the Walcott "eye," precise but at the same time lyric, full of painterly gesture.

And where to start? As there is not much overt meaning to be extracted, I can easily focus on the accumulation of images and atmospheric suggestions. These make a kind of meaning themselves, just not one that can be passed along.

Sepia is the tone of nostalgia, the gone world, images in sepia resonant of all that has been. One does not just feel nostalgia, one indulges it. It is, as per its Greek root, 'the longing for home.' And Walcott's deployment of images suggests as much, though it's obvious, of course, that we are looking at a postcard of colonialism.

Walcott's refraction is complex in itself, but it gets more complex still once we consider Jean Rhys herself. The writer was born in Dominica, West Indies, and lived there until she was sixteen. She only began to publish when she was living in England, and most of her novels, like *After Leaving Mr. MacKenzie* are urban tales of loneliness and love gone wrong (I simplify, of course).

The one exception, and possibly Rhys' most acclaimed novel, is *Wide Sargasso Sea*, which is often described as a prequel to Charlotte Brontë's *Jane Eyre*, for it tells the story of Mr. Rochester's first wife, a Creole woman from the West Indies, who ends up declared insane and locked away in the top floor of Rochester's manse—the fabled "madwoman in the attic." Walcott's poem could then be said to be a kind of prequel to Rhys' novel, showing her as a girl, the writer-to-be, absorbed in Brontë's novel.

~

The poem presents stasis, a *fin de siècle* enervation, the anticipation of what will be the "ax blow" of the new century. Rhys was born in 1890, and in this captured moment she would not yet be ten.

I don't think Walcott is making a strong political indictment here or looking to anatomize the end of empire, though he most certainly serves that up as the implicit context. It seems to me more about the atmospheric saturation that Rhys would take in through her pores and which would then foster the premise of *Wide Sargasso Sea*. And, further, it's about the evocation of that atmosphere by way of the sharpest details tipped in with the most fine-haired brush.

Walcott is, of course, a painter as well as a poet, and his poetic effects often come from his painterly intelligence coming together with his superb ear for the language. Robert Graves famously pronounced that "Derek Walcott handles English with a closer understanding of its inner magic than most…of his English-born contemporaries." The painter's eye is everywhere evident in his visual staging of the scene, and also in his absolute fixation on color, the "tea-brown jungle," the "brown moonlight," the "brown oblivion of an album," counterpointed by the carefully deployed instances of white, or the surprise glimpse of a pink dress disappearing among the jungle green.

This is where I get the thrill, unfailingly I would say. This leads me to propose the idea that real beauty is self-renewing, not to be used up even by repeat exposures. And I find many instances in the poem, all of which then contribute to the larger, gathered-up beauty composed of the separate instances.

The pleasure of the catalogue:

> *they have drifted to the edge*
> *of verandas in Whistlerian*
> *white, their jungle turned tea-brown—*

> ~

> *their features pale,*
> *to be pencilled in:*
> *bone-collared gentlemen*
> *with spiked mustaches*
> *and their wives embayed in the wickerwork*

> ~

> *The green-leaved uproar of the century*
> *turns dim as the Atlantic, a rumorous haze*
> *behind the lime trees, breakers*
> *advancing in decorous, pleated lace*

> ~

> *when the gas lanterns' hiss on the veranda*
> *drew the aunts out like moths*
> *doomed to be pressed in a book, to fall*
> *into the brown oblivion of an album*

Visual specificity—Walcott commands it, here as throughout his work.

And, as must be obvious, visual specificity requires an absolute precision of language: *bone-collared gentlemen with spiked mustaches* and *breakers advancing in decorous pleated lace* and *the gas lanterns' hiss on the veranda drew the aunts out like moths...*

I don't think that it's enough remarked, that almost metaphysical *frisson* the reader experiences when the visual and the sonic coalesce and confirm for us that language used with artistry (Coleridge's "best words in the best order") can capture it—not the world, but our subjective experience of it.

Walcott is usually categorized as a poet and, secondarily, as a painter, the former his vocation, the latter his avocation. And that distinction holds in terms of the mark he left behind and the many honors he received. But in Walcott's creative psyche, they are, it seems, a single gift. I can't think of a poet whose expression draws as deeply on the painterly sensibility. From book to book, his world is *seen*, its landscapes and vegetation, and the ever-varied iterations of the sea. *Jean Rhys* is somewhat of a departure in this regard. The setting here is domestic and nature is kept in the middle distance, present only in some of these distinct spotlit moments.

Ultimately this is a poem about the formation of the writer's sensibility. The panoramic depiction—a colonial world in its last days, a mood of Chekhovian indolence and enervation, an overall sense of night coming on—everything narrows to a point, comes to rest in the image of the young girl who we know will become a writer and who will write a book responding to Brontë's *Jane Eyre*, and the white of the paper. The signifying color has been there throughout the poem, six appearances before this last, which is presented as a culmination, a wedding.

THE EGRET

Peter Campion

In the title poem of Derek Walcott's 2010 collection, *White Egrets*, the birds in question take on various guises. They're those literal creatures the poet observes "gliding over ponds, then balancing on the ridge/of a silken heifer, or fleeing disaster/in hurricane weather..." At the end of the poem they arrive as the "seraphic souls" the poet associates with his friend Joseph Brodsky. In the seventh of the eight sections, most beguilingly, the egrets appear in a metaphor about writing poetry:

> We share one instinct, that ravenous feeding
> my pen's beak, plucking up wriggling insects
> like nouns and gulping them, the nib reading
> as it writes, shaking off angrily what its beak rejects.

That single sentence, embedded in a rhymed quatrain, captivates me.

For one thing, it points to the strengths and subtleties of the whole collection. I have in mind Walcott's blend of verbal wit and gestural embodiment, elegance and bare emotion—including his anger at the "new makers" of the Caribbean, "where yet another luxury hotel will be built / with ordinary people fenced out." Like the egrets, these poems are impelled by bare necessity. They perform their work in the face of mortality.

The lines often show a surprising starkness—as if Walcott were remembering his own "Homage to Edward Thomas" from decades earlier:

> Lines which you once dismissed as tenuous
> Because they would not howl or overwhelm,
> As crookedly grave-bent, or cuckoo dreaming,
> Seemingly dissoluble as this Sussex down
> Harden in their indifference, like this elm.

In *White Egrets*, a similar tone—bare, seemingly tenuous even, then indissoluble—informs the poet's unvarnished portrayal of aging. Take the ninth section of "In Italy":

> In the cool lobby,
> the elderly idle. I am now one of them,
> studying the slow, humped tourists was my only hobby,
> racked now by a whimsical bladder and terrible phlegm.

Sometimes, he sees his creative powers themselves in peril. Consider the ending of poem "19":

The failed canvases
turn their shamed faces to the wall like sins.
A square of sunlight slowly passes
across the studio floor. I envy its patience.

This stringency extends to self-appraisal, as in the third section of "Sicilian Suite":

All of those people and their lucky lives.
I know what I've done, I cannot look beyond.
I treated all of them badly, my three wives.

So, how does *White Egrets* prove a collection of such imaginative generosity? For sure, the raw moments are only half the story: they don't prevent the characteristic Walcottian lushness from surging up, or forestall the humorous scenes, like the second section of "In the Village":

Everybody in New York is in a sitcom.
I'm in a Latin American novel, one
in which an egret-haired *viejo* shakes with some
invisible sorrow, some obscene affliction,
and chronicles it secretly, till it shows in his face,
the parenthetical wrinkles confirming his fiction
to his deep embarrassment.

But the authorial largesse in *White Egrets* derives most of all from the movement of intelligence and feeling in these poems. I mean the way that Walcott's sentences and lines, even in the gravest moments, attend so curiously both to the world and to their own unfolding, as in that canny figure, "the nib reading / as it writes," which he rhymes with the egret's "ravenous feeding."

I'm confident in my judgement of these poems, but my fascination with the figure of the egret remains personal, too, a welcome reminder of what it was like to be Derek's student more than twenty years ago at Boston University. That fall, we met in the small classroom at 236 Bay State Road, a gray stone building often wrapped in fog from the Charles River. The rumor was that Derek got up at 4 AM every day to write, and, sure enough, by the time he arrived, he was often kicking puns around and tinkering with phrases—as when he told us that critics should pay less attention to "the anxiety of influence" and more to "the influence of anxiety."

He was both playful and demanding, and he gave us the most generous thing he could, a boot camp on the poetic line. Our reading ranged through the centuries, always homing in on the felt particulars. He had us all recite, for example, the first line of Emily Brontë's "Remembrance":

Cold in the earth—and the deep snow piled above thee.

Or maybe it was a line from Marlowe's *Tamburlaine*:

And ride in triumph through Persepolis?

It could have been from Keats's "The Eve of Saint Agnes":

The hare limped trembling through the frozen grass.

Or Thomas Hardy's "The Voice":

Woman much missed, how you call to me, call to me.

Or Auden's "The Fall of Rome":

The piers are pummeled by the waves.

Did we hear how good those lines are? Did we understand how they work aurally? Mimetically? Derek sometimes stopped us and had us recite a line again, but this time pronounce only the vowels. He often asked, "if you were a movie director, how would you film this line?"

He had us describe the effects of single words, syllables, letters. The result was the best thing a student of poetry could ask for, an immersion in the bodily intelligence of great poems.

We followed Derek around that fall, from the creative writing program on Bay State Road to the Playwright's Theater on Commonwealth Avenue to the Holiday Inn on Beacon Street in Brookline, where Derek stayed, and where we showed him our poems while sitting in the empty coffee shop with its potted bamboo. There was cantankerous merriment, too—with Derek explaining why Diana Ross was a better singer than Whitney Houston, or analyzing how white college kids screw up the Jamaican accent when they imitate Bob Marley.

Those were exhilarating times, though I remember feeling that, once the banter was over, we'd better not ask too much of Derek, better not linger too long. He had work to do.

I see him wearing suspenders over a pink dress shirt. He's finishing a cigarette outside the entrance to the Holiday Inn and sending us on our way. It must be November because the sycamores are bare. He puts out his cigarette, waves, strolls through the sliding glass and into the dark hotel, intent on something only he knows. That's how I picture him when I read the great opening lines of "White Egrets":

Cautious of time's light and how often it will allow
The morning shadows to lengthen across the lawn
The stalking egrets to wriggle their beaks and swallow
When you, not they, or you and they, are gone. . .

Letters

Rachel DeWoskin & Kirun Kapur

January, 2022

Dear Kirun,

We've been writing to each other for twenty years now: poems, desperate notes, texts, epics on books, teachers, friends, husbands, children, ideas, politics, adventures, joys, sorrows, doubts, academia, rivers, weasels, wombats. But the last time we co-wrote or showed anyone else anything was our letter to the editor at the *NYTimes*, defending Derek Walcott when a colic-stricken reviewer had attacked his poems. We were trying, from the tiny pedestals of youth, to defend Walcott's work. And to say something about who he was to us, as a poet in the world and as our teacher.

Now, from the shores of our forties, our effort reminds me of Didion's hilarious and profound question in "Goodbye to All That" — *was anyone ever that young?* But I also think we were right to write, and to have thought carefully about Derek's poetry while we were in his classroom and for all the years since. Often when I am thinking, reading, swimming, teaching, or writing, I find you in my mind, sorting ideas with me. This is among the greatest joys of my friendship with you, and my life.

I know we're both thinking about Derek's work again during these plague years, and re-reading into it ways to frame the terrifying frailty of human beings. I keep coming back to Derek's idea, which he so often landed on in his workshop and the tumble of years and conversations that followed it: that the problem for poets and students of poetry is that we don't understand love. He meant both in the world and in poems, of course, and also that we, as young writers, weren't able to identify or take the risks necessary to making work that mattered. Those risks were intellectual, political, metrical, and emotional. They had to do with self and other, with landscape, boundaries, and with strangeness and familiarity.

What are the intersections and divergences between sorts of loves – "real" love, 3-D life love, and love in poems? And where do poets fit in? Sometimes I laugh, remembering that Derek called autobiography "a burden on the reader." He also once said of Auden's work, that "the I is not more important than the subject." He loved letters. I loved the letters he wrote us, as his students, and those he wrote Brodsky, of course. His poems often feel like letters – to himself, as well as to others.

There's love between the I and the subject in Derek's poem "Love After Love," which may be read as a letter or even a breakup poem, in the way that Hardy's "Neutral

Tones" may be read as a breakup poem. When we were young, I read it that way, thought we might love, break our own hearts, and smile at ourselves in the mirror as we started up the cycle once more. But now "Love After Love" seems to me to contain wisdom about angling toward repose. What do you take as the poem's suggestion, meaning? Are we — you and I and all of us — capable of love after love? What about the "after", the poem's way of framing time? In this horrifying era, when wonder (once sparkling) feels bleak, will we manage to love the strangers we've become? What say you, my ally in all? Here's the poem, which I know you know, even so. Love, Rachel

LOVE AFTER LOVE

The time will come
when, with elation,
you will greet yourself arriving
at your own door, in your own mirror,
and each will smile at the other's welcome,

and say, sit here. Eat.
You will love again the stranger who was your self.
Give wine. Give bread. Give back your heart
to itself, to the stranger who has loved you

all your life, whom you ignored
for another, who knows you by heart.
Take down the love letters from the bookshelf,

the photographs, the desperate notes,
peel your own image from the mirror.
Sit. Feast on your life.

February, 2022

Dearest R,

A feast, indeed —this poem, your letter. Your words served up a vision of that room where we were young and couldn't know how many years of words would pass between us. I can see the bank of windows and the ring of desks. I always felt the desks were flung against the far wall because Derek was a centrifugal force, lifting us up, flinging us out, until we settled into orbit around him. Once, riding the elevator beside him, I was surprised to note he wasn't actually as large as I'd imagined him to be. He generated so much energy.

I think it's true that we have a meager view of love. In this country, especially, we love romantic love. We valorize maternal love. So many other kinds of love remain unarticulated or mired in the language of self-help. What moves me now about this poem is the way it troubles simple love. It not only suggests that we might "love after love," but also preserves the deep strangeness of that experience. This love isn't glossy or idealized. This love contains exhaustion, loss, and separateness, yet those "unlovely" forces do not undermine the glory of discovery, the joyful shock of seeing yourself and knowing yourself as a stranger. We might still feel "elation," in the midst of misery—at the end of a love or a life. The poem promises, "a time will come…" It promises the possibility that we can keep meeting this stranger, keep experiencing that moment of discovery, that even at the end of things, we remain new.

Strangeness—I'm remembering that Derek loved the idiosyncratic moments in a poem. This was part of his affection for Hardy, wasn't it? The off-note, the unlikely rhyme, the ooze and snarl of grumpiness embedded in a lovely line—the stranger showing up in the mirror. For a poet like Walcott, so capable of perfection in form and image, how interesting that it was the imperfections that interested him. I think you and I are coming to that love, now. Wanting to read work where all the surfaces haven't been sanded smooth. Wanting to preserve, in our own writing, little flashes of what we'd previously have thought of as mistakes. Seeking out the raw, wrong word. Letting the risk show.

What do you think about the form? Perhaps we see a little of that risk, that love for imperfection there—a fifteen-line poem, which could easily have been buffed and smoothed into sonnet? I'll confess the form/body of a poem and the body of a writer/reader/speaker are always connected in my mind. Is a poem without a risk-snarled flaw like a body without a scar? What sort of life can it have lived? How lucky that we found each other's lines and notes and thoughts back then. How lucky that we still get to read and think together, all these forms and tenses later. I'm signing off with one you'll know about another kind of love. Write when you can. Love, K

MIDSUMMER

The jet bores like a silverfish through volumes of cloud—
clouds that will keep no record of where we have passed,
nor the sea's mirror, nor the coral busy with its own
culture; they aren't doors of dissolving stone,
but pages in a damp culture that come apart.
So a hole in their parchment opens, and suddenly, in a vast
dereliction of sunlight, there's that island known
to the traveller Trollope, and the fellow traveller Froude,
for making nothing. Not even a people. The jet's shadow
ripples over green jungles as steadily as a minnow

through seaweed. Our sunlight is shared by Rome
and your white paper, Joseph. Here, as everywhere else,
it is the same age. In cities, in settlements of mud,
light has never had epochs. Near the rusty harbor
around Port of Spain bright suburbs fade into words—
Maraval, Diego Martin—the highways long as regrets,
and steeples so tiny you couldn't hear their bells,
nor the sharp exclamations of whitewashed minarets
from green villages. The lowering window resounds
over pages of earth, the canefields set in stanzas.
Skimming over an ocher swamp like a fast cloud of egrets
are nouns that find their branches as simply as birds.
It comes too fast, this shelving sense of home—
canes rushing the wing, a fence; a world that still stands as
the trundling tires keep shaking and shaking the heart.

March, 2022

Ah, Kirun!

All the nors and nots of those "Midsummer" lines suddenly
stand out to me most, reading them in the context of your
letter and apt, hilarious observation about "the ooze and
snarl of grumpiness embedded in a lovely line."

Derek loved an anapest, yes, an intentional yet
surprising extra foot, the unruly sonnet or chopped off
staccato half-line like the one on which he lands "Love After
Love." The imperative to eat your own life is a five-syllable
affair? This seems to me to be at least a little about his sense

of humor, which you capture in your letter, and which I haven't seen noted that often in the world's conversation about Derek. He was wildly funny. And humor was a sometimes funny, other times stormy force in his classroom and his work, too, for all its seriousness. His joking about identity and love also often took the shape of listing what things were not. Both poems reveal his attentive delineating of presence and absence, maybe a habit having to do with exile, the absence of a once-home, half-lost language, or the ephemera of all human lives. Not to mention the (shared) almost pathological drive of writers to keep track, to make immortal what we know is begging to be broken or lost.

Sometimes here the rhyme feels like a salve, a lullaby gesture of order from the chaos of experience and language. Those very close rhymes: own, stone, Rome, known; shadow and minnow; regrets, minarets, and egrets —give a sense of landing, one if not of safety then at least of a pattern, something we recognize, expect, and come to want, only to land on a sharp, shaking, solo "heart," at the section's end.

This floats up, too, as a record of what's lost, unstable, or coming apart: "no record, nor the sea's mirror, nor the coral busy. . . " and "they aren't doors of dissolving stone," leading to what is, but then *what is* turns out to be pages, coming apart in a damp culture. Even pages come apart, even those love letters he's imploring "you" (himself and us, in my reading) to take down from the shelf, certainly the desperate notes. Our images, too, can be peeled from the mirror. These sorts of coming aparts, peelings, and un-namings, create suspense, a propulsive movement in the poems themselves and a hope in the reader that there may be some putting back together of the broken bits, images, or hearts.

Yet even when we get a version of or gesture toward calm closure such as "sit. Feast on your life," there's still embedded in that a disturbing suggestion of something other than wholeness. Does engaging fully, or loving fully, require peeling our own images from the mirror, recognizing the strangers we are, and then, in the denouement of having achieved such peace, devouring our own lives? Likewise, maybe canefields can be set in stanzas, but at the end, trundling tires will keep shaking and shaking the heart. The shelving sense of home comes too fast, I think, for us to trust it, to think that home, even in the fleeting if life-long container of a human body, isn't reliable. The world stands, though as the trundling tires keep shaking and shaking the heart. Poetry does this too, remains stable though changeable, designed as it is to articulate and accommodate irreconcilable contradictions, including exile, migration, and love.

We memorized so many poems for Derek; do you remember he would make us stand and recite Hart Crane ("The Bridge"), W.H. Auden ("The Fall of Rome"), Thomas Hardy ("Neutral Tones"), and Edward Thomas ("The Owl")? Terror inspired me so acutely that I still remember almost every line; we had to stand in front of our desks like schoolkids and say the poems out loud with Derek stopping us over intonation, a missed word, a voice too quiet to honor its poet, an errant swallow. He was not just funny and sometimes tyrannical, but also theatrical. I remember, and can feel in the lines of both "Love After Love" and "Midsummer," his belief that playwriting, too, was really just poetry on stage, and that poetry deserved to be read aloud, preferably without the sort of self-doubting irony that felt essential to us as twenty-something year-2000 poets. We never wanted to be too wide-eyed, invested, or willing to sing poems, lest our emotional risks overwhelm or humiliate us. But that investment, and that risk, were part of what Derek meant by love. Do you love a poem enough to commit every granular word and breath of it to your heart, and can you speak it with a depth of passion adequate to its life in the world? Are you apologizing for your work in the tone either of the work itself or your reading of it? We are keeping poems alive, both our own and those of others, when we speak or sing or shout them. We are resuscitating what otherwise lies flat on the page when we bring it audibly into a room. So take the risk, say the poem without any apology in your voice, without slouching, whispering, fluttering, or god forbid, chewing gum. Once when I had to recite "The Fall of Rome" for Derek, I had gum in my mouth (I thought this wasn't obvious! What?) and after I finished the poem, flush with the glory of not having missed a single syllable, Derek asked, "Were you auditioning for Guys and Dolls"?

This has been an era full of contradiction, and one of the conflicting senses I have is of a strange and unfamiliar loneliness, something having to do not just with being locked away from one another and our familiar lives and patterns so much in the last few years, but also with the deep divides in our damp culture. At the same time, the fact that everywhere in the world, we are experiencing this plague and its shape-shifting terrors as one species, has made me feel connected to everyone alive and/or who had ever lived (as James Baldwin once described feeling after reading Dickens and Dostoevsky). It cannot be unintentional that at the center, lines 12.5 to 13 of the 25 lines in the section of "Midsummer" you sent is this: "Here, as everywhere else, it is the same age."

I miss our years in Derek's classroom and midst, and I miss him, and I miss you.

Love, Rachel

April, 2022

Dear R,

Yes, I can see us standing in front of those little desks with the fold-up arms, Derek playing the part of the wry, ferocious conductor and critic. He was framed by the windows and the slice of icy river beyond. Terror also motivated me in those recitations (maybe in those days). But, once all our voices were warbling down the lines, a certain pleasure rose up, too. I always felt we were enacting some idea Derek had about the epic nature of all poems—even lyric ones. On the one hand an individual affair—as you say, our singular voices resuscitating the poem lying on the page—and on the other hand, a collective action, a group whose communal voicing served to keep the story of our tribe alive. The sense that a poem, no matter how "autobiographical," lyric, or private it may seem, is a communal act—both when we write it and when we read and recite it—has stayed with me. In lines and stanzas, even us exiles can join and make a people.

Midsummer holds this tension, too, of course. The plane may be landing in place that is removed from "epic" tradition—"a damp culture that comes apart"—a place specific to the poet's biography, but in writing the poem, in reading and speaking it, it joins every, eternal tradition. Those lines, "Here, as everywhere else, it is the same age…Light has never had epochs." Yes, an argument for connection and community, and perhaps even more… for equality. Might real love give us that? Like light, it illuminates everything without prejudice—that which history has celebrated and that which it has excluded. And closer to home, our desperate notes and extra feet, love after love, our glories and our flaws?

Your description of our recitations reminds me of the first time I brought a poem to show Derek in his office (a poem about my own beloved island). He questioned every detail of every line—Why a dash and not a comma? Why break here and not include an extra foot? Why elevate the diction when a simpler word would give it grit? Did I think this word was plain, direct or was it simply lazy? Not knowing how to answer most of his questions, I squirmed and fretted in my seat. Finally, my worry burst and I demanded to know if he could explain his own work in this way. He laughed and said, "No. I'm just checking you're committed." He believed, as you say, we should give our whole selves to poems, even to our mistaken em dashes. He was suggesting a way of paying attention to writing, not unlike memorization. Word by word, pause by pause--an intensity of attention to language that I hadn't known was possible. Yet another kind of love, I think--one that bears down on what it hopes to understand and make, even if that intensity leaves you discomforted.

Thinking about Midsummer now, in relation to our conversation, I'm struck by the fact that it's a kind of letter, too. "Our sunlight is shared by Rome / and your white paper, Joseph". And another favorite from the book begins "Companion in Rome, whom Rome makes as old as Rome." He once described his friendship with Brodsky as friendship between exiles. Brodsky had been teaching at a school near where I'd gone to college. When Derek discovered that I had not sought Brodsky out, he fixed me with a disappointed glare (a lack of commitment!).

Which brings me to some thoughts about "Rome" and your notes on rhyme. One of the lessons I take from Derek's poems involves rhyme's powers: the way rhyme stands against time and creates its own system of meaning. There's such variety of rhyme in this poem—

"own" / "stone" / "known" / "Froude" morphing into "Rome" and finally "home." Here, too, a demonstration of how perfection would not be enough; the imperfect rhyme is also necessary for the poem. The varied rhyme suggests a series of meanings that would not exist without the formal correspondences between the words. We understand the malignant weight of the Froudes of history (with their alleged knowledge) because "stone" and "Froude" and "known" come together in our ear. I love the way "Froude" hovers casting a half-rhyme with "shadow." Then, what was "known" by Froude is transformed by the poet's lines and imagination, so that in the end, the island "home," though it's separated (isolated?) by many lines, finds its equal in its rhyme with "Rome." The chronology of all poems—word following word, one line ticking over into the next—is circumvented by the ability of rhyme to cross the lines and create a simultaneity in our ears and mind—like all our voices reciting together. I also hear a progression from "regrets" / "minarets" / "egrets"…morphing, possibly, into "heart." Do you? Another complication to love—the perfect and imperfect rhymes giving us a regretful, winged, holy, slightly lonely heart.

Love,

K

Bananas of the Mind:
Derek Walcott's Theatrical Imagination

Zayd Ayers Dohrn

The first play I wrote for Derek Walcott's workshop was set in an imaginary zoo. A man and a woman wake up to find themselves in a cage, exhibited like primates in a monkey house. I was 21, probably aspiring to write some kind of mash-up of *No Exit* and *The Hairy Ape*. But Derek was having none of that. "Where do they go to the toilet?" he asked as soon as the reading was over. "Are they supposed to piss on the floor?"

This, to be honest, was a question I hadn't considered. Called out in front of my silent classmates, I murmured something about how monkeys must, in fact, pee in their cages. But this just irritated Derek. "Are your characters monkeys?" he asked. "Because, you know, monkeys don't talk."

This seemed unfairly literal—especially coming from the author of *The Odyssey* and *Dream on Monkey Mountain*, theatrical fever dreams untethered from any kitchen sink naturalism. But when I tried to steer the conversation away from the bathroom, Derek interrupted, again and again bringing the workshop back to these questions of physical reality, and becoming increasingly irritated by my unprepared answers.

Is there a door to this cage? [yes] Is it locked? [yes] What do your characters eat? [bananas?] How do they sleep? [I don't know. On the floor.] Do they bathe? [I guess not] Then wouldn't they start to smell? Doesn't that change the way they would behave? Or at least put a kink in their supposed romance? For all his poetic vision, Derek could be a literalist about the world of the senses.

And I was surprised—that a writer I admired precisely for his riotous theatrical imagination would get hung up on what seemed like simple questions of dramaturgical logic.

But of course, I also wanted to impress him. So my next play was more realistic, set in the bedroom of a teenage boy —an aspiring school shooter—who stockpiles ammunition, takes pills, drinks milk, cuts himself, lifts weights, and uses the toilet (all onstage)—a taxonomy of a character's day-to-day routine. I wanted to show Derek I did in fact understand the mechanics of the human body, the constraints of physical space, the logistics of lived experience.

It didn't work.

"This isn't theatre!" Derek announced at the end of the reading. "If Hamlet could just go on antidepressants and solve all his problems, the play wouldn't be tragedy—it would be a diagnosis."

Again, I argued—I hadn't yet learned my lesson— pointing out that theatrical "madness" transcends diagnosis. That many tragic characters—from Medea to Woyzeck—

suffer from what we would now call mental illness. And that some, in fact—like Oedipus—serve as templates for well-known psychological complexes and disorders. Still, antidepressants would be irrelevant to their stories.

Derek was unimpressed. "Your character," he insisted, "as you've written him? His problems are chemical, not dramatic. A sickness in his brain, not his mind."

Later that year, I got to see Derek's brilliant *Walker*, in a revival at Boston Playwrights' Theatre. The play opens (echoes, again, of *Hamlet*) on a ghostly figure haunting a winter night. For just a moment, I felt vindicated by the supernatural element—where, after all, does a ghost go to the toilet?

But Derek knew better, of course; right away, we find out *his* ghost is hungry:

"I'm as starved as a crow in winter, / cawing on a field fence, / keeping its keen yellow eye / on all who leave and enter."

It soon turns out this "ghost" may be a living person— an assassin, sent by slaveholding interests in the South to silence the press of Black abolitionist printer David Walker. As the scene shifts to Walker and his wife Eliza, they glance out their window to see this apparition prowling the street outside their home:

ELIZA
  I thought I saw something just now,
  like a raven walking in the snow.
  Like a black crow hopping in the cotton;
  but it goes every time I turn.
  I can't see his colour, his face,
  but it been walking round and round
  like a buzzard, circling this place,
  ...

Is he still there? Can you see him?

(Walker goes to the window. Sees him. Lies.)

WALKER
No.

ELIZA
He walks with that slow rhythm
of a crow walking carefully.

WALKER
  I'm sick of this thing.
I see only snow blowing, white air.
It's a blizzard, not a buzzard out there;
it's snowing and the street is dim,
and you see strange shadows in winter.
Come on, you just had a bad dream.

This scene reveals one of Derek's profound gifts as a dramatist—the ability to root his poetic vision in tangible lived experience. The ghostly figure seems real (the stage directions tell us that Walker "sees him"), but then again, he may be just a trick of the eye—"snow blowing, white air,"—or "strange shadows in winter"—or perhaps a bad dream. On the other hand, these explanations may only be the lies Walker tells himself—that we all tell ourselves—when we're tricked by our senses, when we come across something inexplicable, an experience that passes all understanding.

Walker made me understand what Derek had been trying to teach us in our workshop that year—not just about the failure of my own plays, but about his unique idea of theatrical "reality." His plays are never literal, never merely naturalistic, but the visionary in his work—the poetic and the unreal—are always rooted in the physical, in our senses. Ghosts, dreams, visions—all hover, but their unreality— their *ghostliness*—grows out of what is real and tangible —out of our bodies, our eyes, and our ears.

In every play I've written since, I've tried to live up to his standard—to reach for a heightened vision beyond everyday experience, but at the same time to make sure we see the visible—tangible—experience out of which that vision grows.

In *Dream on Monkey Mountain*, Derek gives us this quintessentially Walcottian exchange:

BASIL
I am Basil, the carpenter, the charcoal seller. I do not exist. A figment of the imagination, a banana of the mind…

CORPORAL
Banana of the mind, figment of the … ho! That's pretty good.

And is pretty good—not just as poetry (the play of "banana" and "fig") or as a bawdy phallic joke ("ho! That's pretty good"), but also as expression of an entire aesthetic philosophy.

Because in Derek's plays, the fruits of the imagination are tangible objects—unexpected and out of place, elevated above the everyday, but nonetheless *real*, with their own weight and presence, their own physical sensation. Which may explain why they are so uniquely satisfying to hear, to see, to unpeel, and to taste.

No Winter In It

Martin Edmunds

The scope of Derek Walcott's achievement is challenging to encompass. As he wrote in his essay "What the Twilight Says," on starting out in St. Lucia and later founding a theater in Trinidad:

> The writers of my generation were natural assimilators. We knew the literature of empires, Greek, Roman, British, through their essential classics; and both the patois of the street and the language of the classroom hid the elation of discovery. If there was nothing, there was everything to be made. With this prodigious ambition one began.

I am almost certain Walcott's conviction came, as he said about the Cockney Keats, "from his belief in what he was doing, his faith in poetry, and his knowledge that what matters is the intensity of the focus on the single word." If Walcott's ramifying similes sometimes close in a thicket, in class he interpreted Keats's exhortation "to load every rift with ore" as affirming that "it's better to overdo, be obscure, than for the next line to just continue in the same furrow. Thought is obscure; is chaos. No poem survives that does not confront its own antithesis, its undoing coming from the opposite direction." That turn of thought can arrive quietly or be showy as the volta of a white-cap crashing onshore, the rebound wave rippling outward, but in either case, it creates an undertow. The surface of his poems is sometimes complex, plaited like laid rope, but when he wants, Walcott can be clear as cold brook water, plain as daylight (though it's the wind blowing through his poems that ventilates even the densest of his work and brings renewal):

> When I press summer dusks together, it is
> a month of street accordions and sprinklers
> laying the dust, small shadows running from me.
> . . . .
> There is the Hudson, like the sea aflame.
> I would undress you in the summer heat
> and laugh and dry your damp flesh if you came.
>
>   ("Bleecker Street, Summer")

Derek insisted in poems and plays, in class and conversational asides—and his best work proves—that all of language is mimetic (syllable, word, syntax, rhythms of phrasing, line, sentence, even the shapes of letters, though their sounds are primary) and tied to the body. Listen, but also feel the work your mouth is made to do, how your throat opens, when you read aloud. Try it here, the first quatrain of the first sonnet—each conceived as a condensed chapter of prose—of his "Tales of the Islands":

> The marl white road, the Dorée rushing cool
> Through gorges of green cedars like the sound
> Of infant voices from the Mission School,
> Like leaves, like dim seas in the mind; ici, Choiseul.

Walcott's knowledge of patois, French, Spanish, his love of other poetries of the Caribbean basin and Latin America written in those tongues, of pan, parang, and calypso, and his affection for the poets Aimé Césaire, Saint-John Perse, Octavio Paz, Pablo Neruda, Jorge Luis Borges, brought new dictions and new strains into his own music in English. As in "Sainte Lucie" ("Pomme arac,/otaheite apple"; "Iona") and in "Parang":

> Man, I suck me tooth when I hear
> How dem croptime fiddlers lie,
> And de wailing, kiss-me-arse flutes
> That bring water to me eye!

And in "Cul de Sac Valley," first treated a decade earlier in *Another Life*:

> A panel of sunrise
> on a hillside shop
> gave these stanzas
> their stilted shape.

. . . as consonants scroll
off my shaving plane
in the fragrant Creole
of their native grain;

from a trestle bench
they'd curl at my foot,
C's, R's with a French
or West African root[;]

like muttering shale,
exhaling trees refresh
memory with their smell:
bois canot, bois campêche,

hissing: *What you wish*
from us will never be,
your words is English,
is a different tree.

That take on language as mimetic is productive for a writer, because it links experience to the weight and rhythmic run of words on the page. In Shakespeare's *Henry VIII*, when Cardinal Wolsey learns that he had negligently placed a paper revealing his duplicity in a packet he sent the King, he knows his exalted life is over:

I shall fall
Like a bright exhalation in the evening
And no man see me more.

I took that third line—all monosyllabic words separated by strong word-boundary sounds (consonant cluster, tenuto notes of long, terminal vowels, sustained nasal *n* and liquid *r*) and the run of five strong stresses in six words—to be the meteor's last flames, expiring one by one. More tuned to reality, bolder on how poetry contains time, in class Derek said he read it as the first stars *reappearing* after the meteor has flamed out.

From very early, Walcott could write with measured delight and the cool appraisal of reason, travel the width of the world in four beats to rival Marvell ("In a Green Night"); take on the splendor and wonder, the tone of prophecy, a touch of the wrath of the Bible; be sinewy as Blake ("Pocomania"); gorgeous as Marlowe's mighty, or cut you with the shiv-slivers of that mirror the Elizabethans held up to—be shattered by the Jacobeans. Though not in Kit's stichomythic rhythm, his line by line *gradus ad*, more the sinuous movement and symphony, the sounding together of the whole orchestra in fused verse paragraphs Shakespeare first achieved.

Apart from the epic poem "Omeros" and the book-length "Tiepolo's Hound," others' seismographs might record different heights of sustained ambition and achievement, but most print-outs showing those steep peaks will include "The Schooner *Flight*," "Koenig of the River," perhaps "The Fortunate Traveller," although there's some murkiness concerning how the speaker of this poem—"What was my field? Late sixteenth century./ My field was a dank acre. A Sussex don,/ I taught the Jacobean anxieties"—insinuated himself into the thriller-like deal and betrayal the poem presents. Include, too, without reservation, "The Spoiler's Return" and "The Hotel Normandie Pool." Who can forget Walcott's Ovid, redivivus, who, poolside, "tans his pallor a negotiable bronze," then terry-togaed, speaks:

"When I was first exiled,
I missed my language as your tongue needs salt,
in every watery shape I saw my child,
no bench would tell my shadow, 'Here's your place';
bridges, canals, willow-fanned waterways
turned from my parting gaze like an insult,
till, on a tablet smooth as the pool's skin,
I made reflections that, in many ways,
were even stronger than their origin.
    . . .

"And where are those detractors now who said
that in and out of the imperial shade
I scuttled, showing to a frowning sun
the fickle dyes of the chameleon?
Romans,"—he smiled—"will mock your slavish rhyme,
the slaves your love of Roman structures, when,
from Metamorphoses to Tristia,
art obeys its own order. Now it's time."
Tying his toga gently, he went in.

Like Shakespeare who gave *The Tempest*'s best lines to
Prospero, magus, exiled Duke of Milan, and witch-whelp
Caliban (who tells Prospero, "You taught me language;
and my profit on't/ Is, I know how to curse"): equally
eloquent, each in his own music; so Walcott. You can be
sure of Shabine from "The Schooner *Flight*," that no exiled
Roman poet is going to put him, shinnying sunwards up
the mizzen, in the shade:

Christ have mercy on all sleeping things!
From that dog rotting down Wrightson Road

to when I was a dog on these streets;
if loving these islands must be my load,
out of corruption my soul takes wings.
. . . .
I had no nation now but the imagination.
After the white man, the niggers didn't want me
when the power swing to their side.
The first chain my hands and apologize, "History";
the next said I wasn't black enough for their pride.
. . . .
                    "Sir, is Shabine!
They say I'se your grandson. You remember Grandma,
your black cook, at all?" The bitch hawk and spat.
A spit like that worth any number of words.
But that's all them bastards have left us: words.

Walcott wrote poems and plays with characters who
speak coarsely as kings or with the sly sophistication
of a Ti-Jean, a nobody in a folk tale who bests the devil
(heir of Odysseus-Outis, who blinded the Cyclops). In
his playwriting class, Derek spoke of drama's need for
something of the vulgar, street-wise, common, colloquial—
else where get the grit, the traction needed for take off when
the moment for flight arrives? That vulgarity, of the people,
has to be instinctual. "More interesting to be a caterpillar
than to fly. Stay down," he'd tell me. "Casual. Don't pitch
it high; load it with stones, it will rise. Cocteau said, 'In
the theater, you don't write lines, you write rope.' " What
Walcott learned from drama only strengthened his poetry:
poems as much as plays are a performance whose first
duty is to delight. Not separate from what he learned from
the lives of the poor in St. Lucia and Trinidad: life itself is
a performance. That all you got? Step *up*. Asked in class

what he meant by memorable language, finding the right pitch, he told us he'd just been talking in New York with a young actor who said he was about to work with Roscoe Lee Browne. "Terrific. How's that feel?" "I'd rather steal a spoon from the Last Supper than mess up that man."

"Every correct verb is a rhyme; every verb provokes an echo. But so much contemporary verse is so flatly pitched, so prosaic, it provokes no echo. There's no instinct toward memory. The penalty of democracy is there's no care for what was done before. In art, modesty is egotism—it's not about you, in any case. The more you pay the debt to what inspires you, the more you are yourself. A poem is not speech, not conversation. It's a performed music; nobody talks music. The meter of any poem is not arbitrary, it's inevitable. Otherwise it's a lie. To strengthen your thought, contract the line so there's no padding. Rhyme makes you discover an idea superior to reason that contains reason. Read everything. The goal is a mind so various that emphasis on the verb is instinctual."

It ought to be said that the magnitude of his gifts was matched by his generosity—in sharing his knowledge of poetry with students; in the modes opened to other writers by his work; in expecting student writers to hold their own poems, as he did his, to the highest standards; with his time; and with other resources as well. He used his MacArthur grant to turn a storefront building at BU into a black box theater, inviting grad students in the School of Architecture (his son Peter was one) to work with him and come up with the design; he paid professional actors to put on public staged readings and productions of plays by students in his playwriting classes.

Omeros and *The Odyssey* are immense and rightly celebrated, but I am also drawn to the first portraits and sketches of the casts of characters who move through

"Tales of the Islands" and later, Troy Town in *Another Life*, Emanuel-Odysseus, Helen-Janie, Philomène, Ajax the stallion: "the stars of my mythology." Walcott's first book-length poem, *Another Life* may be a seedbed of poems that found fuller expression in subsequent books, but there's a freshness to much of it that has not been surpassed, perhaps especially the portrayal of Anna and first love, making each dawn the first day of the world. This has the lift of Meredith's "Love in the Valley," without the lilt of the dipodies—calmer, slower, golden. It's rare for one writer to play both Homer writing his culture's epic, and his culture's Adam discovering names for its new world he's so soon to lose:

> I asked her, "Choose,"
> the amazed dusk held its breath,
> the earth's pulse staggered,
> she nodded, and that nod
> married earth with lightning.
>
> And now we were the first guests of the earth
> and everything stood still for us to name.
>
> > (*Another Life*, Chapter 13)

Updated in "Adam's Song" from *Sea Grapes*:

> [. . .] men still sing the song that Adam sang
> against the world he lost to vipers,
>
> the song to Eve
> against his own damnation;
> he sang it in the evening of the world

with the lights coming on in the eyes
of panthers in the peaceable kingdom
and his death coming out of the trees,

he sings it, frightened
of the jealousy of God and at the price
of his own death,

the song ascends to God who wipes his eyes:

"Heart, you are in my heart as the bird rises,
heart, you are in my heart while the sun sleeps,
heart, you lie still in me as the dew is,
you weep within me, as the rain weeps."

It's easy to be clinically distant in poetry, in subject,
diction, and tone, especially once you've mastered the
craft of verse. To be this simple and exposed is radical
innocence; such a song of experience and innocence, of
human love—a shock to God—proves to be, as Herbert
says of prayer in his first poem of that title, an "engine
against the Almighty"—engine gentle as the misting of
an eye. Then, too, Herbert's poem isn't simply a list of the
properties or benedictions of prayer, it's an upward cascade,
a rising hierarchy. The pinnacle, past "Church bells beyond
the stars heard, the soul's blood / The land of spices," is
"something understood"—which is also true, including
the cost, of "Adam's Song."

Mercurial poetry. Or rather, more watery than Wa'er
Ralegh's (whom Derek described in conversation as "*silkier*
than Donne"), taking on the tinge, the mineral glint and
taste of all it touches, the shapes of what it fills, or what clay
carafe, what punted Jeroboam it first had been decanted

from for the delectation and enrichment of his ear (i.e., adopting Auden's style in his elegy for Auden). He can have you laughing, two beats later break your heart in English—as in "Summer Elegies," the section that starts "Nothing hurts as much as the word 'California'":

> There's sometimes more pain in a pop song than all
>   of Cambodia,
> and that's the trouble, the heart puts love above it
> all, any other pain—Chernobyl, a mass murder—
> the world's slow stain is there; we cannot remove it.
>
> The irony of it, Cynthia, is that we can never own a-
> nother heart. I must smile or die, hence this lightness.
> Hence this fake chic, these stanza windows like a posh
>   boutique
> in a semitropical desert. Shall I stop the jokes and speak
> for the soul? Soul, was she not your fair and final
>   brightness?

—Or in patois: on a sixteen-seater transport in St. Lucia, returning from walking the streets of the town where he was born to his hotel in "The Light of the World," listening to Marley rocking on the stereo and "lusting in peace" until:

> An old woman with a straw hat over her headkerchief
> hobbled towards us with a basket; somewhere,
> some distance off, was a heavier basket
> that she couldn't carry. She was in a panic.
> She said to the driver: *"Pas quittez moi à terre,"*
> which is, in her patois: "Don't leave me stranded,"
> which is, in her history and that of her people:
> "Don't leave me on earth," or, by a shift of stress:

"Don't leave me the earth" [for an inheritance];
"*Pas quittez moi à terre*, Heavenly transport,
Don't leave me on earth, I've had enough of it."

Her corner of earth was the same one Derek homed to, where salt winds lift off the sea, threshing trees hush the sunset by saying their names: bois flot, bois canot, bois campêche. There are other kinds of achievement and awards for them, including the Nobel Prize, but how many in the last century so refreshed poetry in English? Contenders are few.

I can't close these thoughts without calling attention to *Midsummer*. One favorite poem for Brodsky starts by remembering Quevedo's sonnet *Buscas en Roma a Roma, ¡O Peregrino!*: "Companion in Rome, whom Rome makes old as Rome." Careful!—the indexed first lines hum to keep you up at night if you don't leave the book in another room. And from *The Star-Apple Kingdom*, how not mention "Egypt, Tobago," its swerves and angular cuts among lust, ambition, love, culminating in a "sleep, whose peace / is sweet as death":

Shattered and wild and
palm-crowned Antony,
rusting in Egypt,
ready to lose the world
to Actium and sand,

everything else
is vanity, but this tenderness
for a woman not his mistress
but his sleeping child.

The sky is cloudless. The afternoon is mild.

If this were a film, we'd cut to a shot of Cleopatra and her view of Antony (from the final scene of Shakespeare's play):

His voice was propertied
As all the tuned spheres, and that to friends;
But when he meant to quail and shake the orb,
He was as rattling thunder. For his bounty,
There was no winter in't; an autumn 'twas
That grew the more by reaping. His delights
Were dolphin-like; they show'd his back above
The element they liv'd in.

In Walcott's *Another Life*, the poet portrays his friend Gregorias, a painter. Derek wrote the way he says Gregorias drew—

with the linear elation of an eel.

DARKROOM WATERCOLOR

Thomas Sayers Ellis

This tide of memory begins, of all places, at the top of the Egyptology Building in poet Michael S. Harper's office at Brown University. Sharan Strange and I had taken a bus from Boston to Providence, Rhode Island to ask Harper if he would read in a sort of living room salon that we were starting in a rented Victorian in Cambridge. And although he did not agree to read in our inaugural series and would not read until 1993, it was a terribly successful trip because that day, he talked so much about The Tradition, gave us both free signed copies of his books, allowed me to take his photograph and made us a mini list of poets to contact. When we were leaving he said, "Have you asked Derek Walcott to read yet?"

"No," we said.

"Well, go see him and tell him I command him like a West Indian General to read in your series."

As homage to tradition, the finish line of duty kept us going but this time we walked: left off of Inman onto Mass Ave, through Central Square, past MIT, across the bridge above the body of water that has been punished to pretend it's a river and the sea, a glance at the raised neon Citgo pyramid along its banks then (as if led by the angel of geometry) a right turn onto Bay State Road. Look at it this way: Before the age of thirty, it is (perhaps) best to discover poetry with one's legs rather than one's heart.

We did not make an appointment in advance because we did not want to telegraph our intentions which might have been misinterpreted (depending on mood) as a literary handout. Our mission was to see Derek Walcott, meet him, hear his voice in the same reef-building corals of air as our own voices. We did not want to call him on the phone and say, "We're starting a Reading Series in our house and we would like for you to read but we have no money to pay you." No, this had to be done, face to face, eye to eye. The noose of persuasion had to become a conjunctive ampersand and the conjunctive ampersand had to become the serpent making yet another thread of associations between nouns. I had my begging knife ready in case he said No. And to get the job done, I was committed to becoming the smiler next to him armed with an artillery of arguments (not a coat) of many colors. Scansion (that ol' castrator of lines) must have been on our side that day, because when we arrived his office door was slightly opened and he was sitting behind his desk. A knock. "Come in."

"Hi Mr. Walcott, I'm Thomas Sayers Ellis and this is Sharan Strange and we came from Cambridge to ask if you would read in our literary series."

"You two came all the way from Harvard to ask me to read?"

"Yes, Sir"

"Tell me about the Series."

"It's for Black Writers. Each reading is a pairing of emerging and established Black Writers.

"I'm not a Black Writer."

"I don't care. I just want you to read your poems in our Series."

"Who will you pair me with?"

"A local writer, a poet-lawyer, Martin Espada, and when I asked him to read, he said the same thing, I'm not a Black Writer."

Silence

"Sharan, tell him what Michael Harper said."

Sharan delivered the verbal mail sent by the big man in the beret, the man in the ivy castle, he who would be something of a Charles Mingus if Mingus had not already been Mingus, the Poet Laureate of Rhode Island, and that's when the interior of Derek's face, like a massive spy behind flesh, the metaphor beneath the mask, convinced the exterior of his face to abandon the prolific profile of similes and that's when "a cool air of change" occurred reaching the shores of his expression and a smile was born. If you have never seen this, I direct your attention to the illustration on the cover of *Collected Poems 1948–1984* (Faber and Faber).

Did you ever sit, eye-to-eye, with *that* Derek, the folly-filled Cheshire Comrade who knew how to hide his need for appreciation in the creative and secretive layers of an inner tide, the Walcott whose soul no camera or focusing of external eyes could take, reject or drown? When I asked him if I could take his photograph to use for publicity and the program, he said Yes and (still seated) turned his head toward me, replacing the expression of a shrewd bard with a moment of author-photo-gentleness.

It's hard to properly photograph a poet, especially if the photographer is also a poet, particularly a younger poet and the poet being photographed is an older, more established poet only a decade or so away from being awarded the Nobel Prize for Literature. Throw in admiration, respect, awe as well as a trojan horse of Black poet fear and there is absolutely no possible way that the resulting image will be a truly inspired collaboration. At best, the entire roll of film, as if nervously scribbled in pencil, will be sloppily filled with the visual equivalent of a high schooler's sketchbook.

The date of the reading was approaching and I hadn't heard from him, no follow up, no acknowledgement, no return call. I was getting nervous and, having nothing concrete to go on but the agreement in his office, the word of a poet between poets, I wasn't fully convinced that the commitment was solid. And yet we went ahead with the Fall 1989 Schedule, thinking that the printed word would make the event a reality. I developed the photograph that I took of him in the very small darkroom at the top of our house and once I saw it, the wet-ish eyes, several feathers (momentarily) returned to my plucked hope.

And still, there was only one thing to do, bum rush his home. I knew where he lived but have no idea, currently, how I knew. Another trip, this time just me. The #1 bus to Back Bay, an hour in the Avenue Victor Hugo Bookshop where the poet Sam Cornish (all afro and glasses, nearly Robert Hayden-esque) worked and loved to talk. After that: resistance! Walk by the yellow and red bags spilling out of Tower Records without allowing a single dollar in my wallet to participate in the suicide of spending. Yes, as well as paper poets, there was paper money in those days. Then walk down Commonwealth Avenue through Kenmore Square to the Boston Book Annex—all that praying into books just to resurrect my paginated nerves.

Buzzer, knock. Lord knows this could blow up in my face. Knock again, don't leave, wait.

He came to the door in a robe, welcomed me in, and before I spoke said, "Wait here." Me and my bag of books, a full leather satchel (on my back) and an indifferent plastic bag, standing there waiting to be turned into stone. That's the photograph the whole sky might have caught were I holding a Sunday lemon in one hand and a last supper of sea grapes in the other but no, all I had were used books waiting to die and become one of them—akin to the end of "Summer Elegies," a victim of my own rudeness for showing up, again, without permission. When he returned, he was carrying a type-written manuscript and handing it to me, he said, "There it is: my last book. I'm done." I thought. Whoa, as I held the weightlessness of paper light and Shabine (throughout the surf of my flooding throat) kept his promise to Shine, his past self, wading in the mythology of the resurrection hidden in every reference, blowing out yet another candle; and Derek, seeing that I did not want to tongue-butcher the title, pronounced it for me, "Omeros." His last book, well, I did not believe him but I immediately thought maybe, just maybe, he was standing there in his robe saying not that he had nothing else to say and not that poetry was finished with him but that he was dying. Opening the manuscript and there, in the first stanza, was the annoying trinity of "sunrise," "cameras" and "news."

Then one of us (I hope it was me) started the social editing process of making sure I wasn't there long, so I reminded him about the reading, which he had forgotten. And I gave him a copy of the Series schedule that mimicked a paper broadside. He said he would just be arriving back in Boston that evening and would come directly from the airport. I couldn't believe that I did not believe him but had to believe him, the thing he said and the thing he had not—his facts and my fiction. I had just held the last book of a dying man who was not dying. However, there would be four more volumes of poetry, a huge prize, Sir attached to the sunrise of his name and the letters KCSL OBE and OCC attached to the sunset of it. However, had I known I would not have told him nor would I have mentioned the rectangular plot on Morne Fortune, the one within the margins of the picket fence made of short, white guardian obelisks or the final chapter of living verse that (at a different level of artistry) becomes the first chapter all over again. A vague sadness like a bit of a blank, organic sheet of paper is how I felt and saw myself standing on the steps as I left. Perhaps one of those celestial Egyptians in a canoe would offer me a ride and we would both float up toward Brookline to another used bookstore.

It was nighttime when he walked through the door of our house and, as I recall, he missed Espada's reading and we were already in the break between readers and stalling. Trench coat, slip on dress boots, the November of New England looking for ways to attach charters and cold cuts to the warmth of Saint Lucian loosh. "Walcott's here," both Danielle Legros Georges and John Keene found me to say. *The Arkansas Testament* was his most recent book at the time so I had hoped he would read from it but Derek being

Derek, decided to sit the entire reading and turn the clock back to 1973's *Another Life*. He read continuously without break or commentary for 40 to 45 minutes then said, "Thank You." Not used to that: the sitting, the one long poem. We were used to being engaged between poems—laughter, commentary, references to The Struggle, call and response, the performance of a literary church of sorts, references to the same physical home (or one close to it) that we were from, our own brand of code-knowing and code making.

Of course, too, there was more than a bit of drama. Someone said they were called a Spic and a few years later that same someone called me Agni's New Nigger. It was a hell-of-a-time to be a Black, Brown, Light-skinned or Interracial poet in Boston and Cambridge. I know that this is not the kind of thing you expect to hear in this space but it is language that belongs to the charged atmosphere of that period as a new generation of the victims and victors of Identity Politics were tossing narratives from the "I" of their hearts into the sky of publishing, writing workshops and readings hoping something would stick. It was a great night! Patrick Sylvain videotaped it. If there was any twilight left after the reading worth listening to then its mischievous twin, the one with the more lyrical mouth, hid till breakfast. Derek once told me, "Don't compete with your contemporaries. Compete with the dead, those who came before you."

During the summer of 1994, the sun squeezed three or four stingy water-colored sonnets out of July. A few of us are standing outside the Huntington Theater in Boston. It is intermission. We have been watching The Trinidad Theater Workshop's production of *Dream On Monkey Mountain*. Raised above the street level near the entrance of the theater, students and writers are smoking and chatting. Would you like a roll call of who is in the photograph, no fucking way, but I will say that there is a line (of poets) around Derek, broken, and pretending not to be a line. Derek is finally alone. I am a graduate student in the Creative Writing Program at Brown University but since Derek has extended the use of the Boston Playwrights' Theater to the Dark Room Reading Series for our 94-95 season, I have come to see Dream and to show my appreciation. Looks like he is wearing linen, looks like he's leaning toward possibly saying yes if I ask him if I can sit in on his graduate writing workshop at Boston University in the Fall. Already my mind is riffing on the related possibilities of the linguistic likenesses of his response. It could be a No-No (like in baseball), could be Noa Noa (as in Gauguin) or it could be (given the mixture of accents) Noah Noah, a stuttering call to the man who let the whole world die.

"Hey Derek, the play is wonderful work and that actor Wendell Manwarren is amazing!"

"Yes. Thank you."

"I was wondering if I could ..."

Intermission Over

I showed up on the first day of class anyway and told him that he said yes when I asked him if I could sit in. What did you think I was going to do? Of course, I lied but let's call it the theater that occurs outside of the theater, an opportunity. I wanted to be in the class. And I knew, from years of working in bookstores, running a reading series, and hanging out with older writers how the literary career ladder worked. First statement, first day of class, "If you use a computer to write your poems, please leave" after which he talked about the relationship of the hand to the eye to the brain in writing. And he gave us a poem to memorize, "The Fall of Rome" by W.H. Auden. I did well on the memorization. The next week I had a one on one with him. I gave him a poem. He read it, said it was fiction (not poetry), gave it a rip and returned it to me in a crumpled ball. "It's ok I have another copy," I said but he was right. The poem was extremely uninspired, a page-proceeding service to nothing deserving of service. A retelling of an experience, a linear stone echo. "Rewrite it," he said. I did but I also began to find it more and more difficult to make the weekly commute from Providence to Boston.

In 1998, I invited him to read at Case Western Reserve University where I taught in the English Department. On the way from the airport, he said, "I saw a poem by you in one of those Best American things. It was good." Immediately, I stopped the car and threw my hands up and shouted, "Derek liked my poem!" Back for another quick tour of duty, that Cheshire Comrade grin scanned the passenger seat's windshield for the muse of moths. A spondee in slacks. Sometime after lunch and before the reading, I photographed him out in the April sun of the Coventry section of Cleveland Heights, a few times alone and a few times with Karen Job, a local poet from the Caribbean who knew and loved Derek's poetry. They spoke as if they were recording reggae and I saw and heard a side of Derek that I had not witnessed before. A few years later when I read with him and Yusef Komunyakaa at The Painted Bride in Philadelphia, I mentioned that she died of Cancer and it shook him. To this day, I can't find the negative, the coated, sheet of plastic castaway. Karen Job, one of those "cities that passed us by on the horizon."

Much is made of the silences between stanzas, but sometimes, as is the case of "Midsummer, Tobago," the shutter (without the harsh and critical interruption of flash) clicks at the end of every line till the old world, disguised as its foe, the new world, is unrecognizable. No one knows this more so than the tourists who try to take Philoctetes soul with their cameras at the beginning of *Omeros*. In one form (or medium) or another, they are always as present as the mountain behind its photographer's shroud in "The Lighthouse" or the news photograph of the glowing, candle-white corpse on a cold altar in "Che." For Derek, the artificial light of the tourist seemed always present, sometimes shapeshifting into a souvenir-hungry reader and sometimes shapeshifting into a shipwrecked listener.

At the beginning of the reading in Cleveland, while checking the microphone, a woman seated in the front row rather hurriedly took a photograph of him and he walked off the stage and said a few words to her and then he returned to the podium and said, "Everybody has quirks but flash photographs really throw me if I am reading, so please... don't." I was also on the front row but could not hear what he said to her as it was done with the same "grace of effort" that he spoke about in *The Antilles*. I also got my wish (without asking) as he read exclusively from *The Arkansas Testament*, the small, light blue Faber edition. The bird on the cover flies to the right (leaving North) while the bird on the cover of *The Fortunate Traveler* glides to the left (leaving South). One away from the other. Flight, like "love, made seasonless."

"I am going to read mainly from a book called *The Arkansas Testament* and I don't know why. You go on different readings and I was just in North Carolina. And you have a sensation, a feeling that perhaps this would go down better than other things. You forget, sometimes, what you've written and to look at what you did write can produce some terrible reactions of embarrassment, perhaps even a little bit of pride sometimes. I think the poems that

I've chosen today primarily have a kind of directness that I like to convey."

Derek won the Nobel Prize for Literature in 1992, the prize is named for Alfred Bernhard Nobel, the man who invented dynamite. And if I had to pick a photograph of him that is most emblematic of a Nobel Laureate, I would choose the black and white image that appears on the back of the cloth edition of *Midsummer*. Taken in 1982 by Tom Victor, does he not look the part of the archaic poet who has screwed more than a few continents to his eye? A flame of hair burning the side of the face, almost as much of a peninsula as Italy, a gossipy gull serenading a canal of mustache. The eyes, preservers of light, biographic islands.

A Secret Correspondence

Carolyn Forché

When Derek Walcott's poetry first came into my hands, his *Another Life*, I was in my twenties, and had not yet encountered poetry such as this, *where the pages of the sea/ are a book left open* and the moon *whitewashed the shells/ of gutted offices barnacling the wharves/ of the burnt town.* This was a poetry where *Bible-papered voices/fluttered shut," and the drizzle shivered its maracas, /like mandolins the tightening wires/of rain,* and where the sea was legible in the pages of its waves, and barnacle had become a verb. Walcott's diction was an astonishment.

Mine was the flat-vowelled plain speech of the upper Great Lakes. Our poetic language was a sack of stones, stars, and snow, and in the nest of a bird could sometimes be found the skeleton of a bird, but nothing stranger than that. Our poems made few arguments. They were propelled by instances of perception— often visual— that might, if we were fortunate, achieve what the *Imagistes* called a "vortex": whirlpools of connotative and tropic meaning, or so we hoped, even though we were not then much influenced in other respects by the *Imagistes*. Ours was the poetry of "the middle voice": simple in diction, even-toned, lineated in syllabics, with occasional attention to the drama of enjambment. As we eschewed rhetorical abstraction, we were left without very much to say beyond *road*, *wood*, and *grave*.

Walcott described things as *lacertilian, chiton-fluted, medaled by pellets of sheep dung*. From him I learned *mattock, cerecloths, shallop, pirogue* and *blent*. He took me to *Soufrière, Anse-la-Raye, Sauters*, to the *Canaries* and *Choiseul*, and in his poems I tasted the fruits: *goyave, corrosol, bois-canot, sapotille*. Reading Walcott's poetry for the first time, I *put the shell's howl* to my ear and heard a new English, threaded with Latin and French, a world English bringing colonized peoples to life on paper and dredging the murk of history, a deep night punctured with the *sidereus* light of poetry and art. This personal lyric memoir of loves and friendships, warfare, enslavement, and colonization—is an autobiography at once personal, historical and mythic. It moves through childhood to Walcott's middle age, sailing the archipelago of the Windward Islands of the West Indies, mapping his natal Saint Lucia, beautiful and blood-soaked and named (it is said) by shipwrecked sailors. An island inhabited by the Arawaks, then the Caribs, that came to be ruled seven times each by the British and the French, an agon that caused the jewel, Saint Lucia, to be compared with Helen of Troy.

His language became my lodestar, but it would be some years before I would meet Derek Walcott in person. I don't remember precisely when or where the first meeting took place. In memory we are walking in a city on a winter night among poets who have just read together somewhere. New York or Cambridge. A light snow is falling. My reading was from a work-in-progress, *The Angel of History*, still several years from publication. The group may have included Allen Grossman, so we could have been coming from Blacksmith House. Or Joseph Brodsky was there that night, and we were in New York. Derek was walking beside me, talking about the poetic line, the music and compression of the line as it defied the gravity of syntax. Here the delicate memory bursts like a globe of breath and is lost. There would be other encounters at poetry events. We would receive an award together in Pittsburgh, we would draft a resolution in Key West condemning the first invasion of Iraq. In between, he invited me to be his interlocutor on a television book show focused on his re-imagining of Homer's Odysseus—his *Omeros*, the seeds of which germinated in *Another Life*, wherein he introduced the possibility of transposing various St. Lucians upon the figures in Homer's epic, sending the ships of the island called "Helen of the West" to the open sea.

We were serendipitously invited to join many poetry conferences and festivities, and always he would pull me aside to talk about poets—Francis Ponge, W.H. Auden, Anna Akhmatova, Paul Celan—and also his ideas regarding prosody, most particularly his measure of the poetic line. He was by turns serious and playful, with an irreverent, ribald sense of humor. He was also courtly, sarcastic, and self-deprecating, and he used the N-word often. "You will win the Nobel,' I told him over lunch in the Algonquin Hotel following our televised conversation regarding

Omeros. "No, I will not. They have already given the Nobel to a N-word," and he laughed derisively. I told him that I disagreed. The other giants, Octavio Paz, Joseph Brodsky and Czeslaw Milosz had already been awarded the Nobel Prize. Derek's would come between Nadine Gordimer and Toni Morrison, and soon a fifth poet, Seamus Heaney, would follow—in the time when giants walked the earth, the time the Swedes still refer to as "the era of poets."

One year, Derek asked me to come to Saint Lucia in January, together with Milosz, Brodsky, Heaney and maybe a few others. We would feast, swim in her sea, walk her beaches and talk about poetry. Would I accept to come? It was the chance of a lifetime, a chance to be in the presence of the giants in a tropical paradise. At the time I was the mother of a young child, with a job at an unforgiving university, so I had to decline his invitation. Derek was certain that this was the moment for me to visit, that it was the right thing for me to do. He would show me his Saint Lucia, his Castries, the harbor of his survival, but no, it was impossible, and the chance would not come again. In that winter, I did not yet know of the fleetingness of life, as I do now. In that winter, I could not have known what I was giving up.

One summer, we were both invited to the Aspen Writers Conference, before or after the missed chance to see Saint Lucia. Surrounded by the still snow-capped peaks, the poets picnicked under flotillas of hot air balloons. "You mentate too much, Forché," he said, "you need something to lift you out of your thoughts." He suggested painting in watercolors, a medium he had mastered. He corralled me to accompany him to an art store in Aspen to buy half-pans of watercolor pigments, brushes and other supplies. I followed him through the aisles as he chose what would be right for me: cadmium red, yellow ochre, Phthalo green, ultramarine, azo yellow, new gamboge, alizarin crimson, a black, and a neutral gray. "You need a forgiving paper," he said. A paper that would forgive me.

With colors, brushes, and a quart of water we settled on the mountainside for a lesson in paying attention to light and shadow. After wetting the sheets of paper before us, we looked upon the mountains with clouds above them, and the herds of Charolais grazing in the meadow grass. "Look at the light, Forché," he instructed, and not at the cows. Paint the light. Pay attention to the shadows that define the light." I brushed grey wash upon the soaked surface of the paper and attempted as best I could to suggest mountains. "You are not looking at the light!" he protested, "you are trapped in forms and the outlines. You must first paint the light." And it went like that: my nervous brush, too much water, undefined pigment and absorbent paper, a chaos of gestures. It was, as both of us realized, hopeless. I was not a painter. But I was, he insisted, a poet, and that meant more to me than anything else would have done. We stayed beneath the hot air balloons that floated beside the mountains, while Derek painted the clouds, brushed the peaks into shape with water, and in the meadow somehow positioned the cows as more than watery suggestions, all the while reciting lines of poetry he loved. When he invited me to do the same, I remembered the passage I most loved from *Another Life: And I answer, Anna, /twenty years after, /a man lives half his life. /The second half is memory,//the first half, hesitation/for what should have happened/ but could not, or//what happened with others/when it should not.* He was surprised that I knew him by heart.

As each of Derek's books appeared, I obtained two copies: a hardcover for the groaning shelf dedicated to his work, a papercover to underline and fill with marginalia. Early on, Robert Graves, whom I'd met in Deya, Mallorca, proclaimed: "Derek Walcott handles English with a closer understanding of its inner magic than most (if not any) of his English-born contemporaries." His friend, Joseph Brodsky, later wrote: "For almost forty years throbbing and relentless lines kept arriving in the English language like tidal waves, coagulating into an archipelago of poems without which the map of modern literature would effectively match wallpaper. He gives us more than himself or 'a world'; he gives us a sense of infinity embodied in the language."

This sense of mathematical infinity is echoed in Walcott's own reflection: "The anguish of every art is that it is continually groping to escape from itself. Van Gogh would have plastered thick sunlight onto his Provence canvasses instead of pure paint, if he could. Language, especially in the form of poetry, gropes for an algebraic precision, in which letters have the unchanging rigidity of numbers." However this may be so, Walcott also believed that poetry begins in induced chaos, in accident as illumination, error as truth, typographical mistakes as revelation. Poetry does not begin in self-conscious intention. Walcott once quipped: "I cannot think because I refuse to, unlike Descartes. I have always put Descartes behind the horse, and the horse is Pegasus."

This playfulness brings me to the matter of a certain secret correspondence. During years of intense travel on both our parts, our friendship took an epistolary turn when I began receiving letters, undated, from a certain "Kurt" written to me as "Helga," a penname he had created. I knew they were from Derek, as he had previously introduced these alter-egos in conversation. I found several of the letters recently, while going through the museum of my life, and as this side of him might not be known otherwise, I will share an excerpt. It seems he imagined that we were engaged in international espionage, with secret rendezvous and Swiss accounts.

Dear Helga,

I am writing to you from the white slopes of the Platz mountains, watching the skiers...and thinking pure thoughts like snow, and most of all I am remembering the war. When you left me right there on the dock, while all the...arrows were flying around our heads like sharp similes. I thought I would never see you again and I have not. How far away is Switzerland, Austria, anywhere from the turmoils and skirmoils we have seen. I remember you in your pith helmet and your courage and I remember my pith pants....How brave you were, how noble, how nobel, how pleasant, how pulitzer, how often I think of you, my fierce little Austrian wombat in combat, reciting Ranny Rilke to an adoring crowd....When I was wounded you balmed me, when I was well you wounded me and touched me with your eyes' artillery, a metaphor as it were. Now, on the white slopes of the Platz mountains, your lion-coloured eyes, your brawny hair, and your two or three warts come rushing down my brains like a mountain torrent a simile never mind. Where is the little marmoset that shared our tent? He must be a guerrilla by now, fighting for Donald Justice for all. I look at the Alps. You look at this. I have gone on too long, but dawn is coming. How still the pines are in the dawn a weak image as it were. I have put your money away quite safe in the Swiss numbered account as we agreed. I am also voting for you as Vice-President some enchanted evening. In the meantime, my lost lioness, my missed marmoset, my talkative mountain torrent, my hope, my Helga, I clutch your babble and your bauble to my heart, and if we never meet again, I can only say what everybody in these cold parts say, Auf Weidershein, meaning it's all the same to me.

Kurt (not to mention Abrupt)

There was never a return address, so Helga never wrote back. There was no Helga. There was only a poet who had once come upon *Another Life*, and saw what poetry could do, even in the present world, in the hands of a master.

DEREK: A FEW NOTES

Jonathan Galassi

What I remember most about Derek is being in St. Lucia, at his airy, serene house at Gros Islet overlooking Pigeon Island, eating breakfast on the terrace, or swimming and having lunch on the beach down the road (though he wasn't much for exercise). Or, more spectacularly, at the wilder beach on the east coast at Cas-en-Bas, the one so beautifully portrayed in his painting reproduced on the cover of the magisterial 2014 gathering of his poems edited by Glyn Maxwell.

On the ride from the airport you passed "Micoud and Dennery, / Then, to leeward, softly, ...Anse La Raye,

Canaries,/Soufrière, Choiseul, Laborie, Vieux-Fort" and experienced yet again how the names of these ordinary if beautiful villages had become the sound of his poetry, taken on incantatory, immortal life in the most perfect verse of our time. It's no exaggeration to say that Walcott forged the conscience of his place, that he is the Omeros of his nation. "My country heart, I am not home till Sesenne sings," he sings, about the great Sesenne Descarte, St. Lucia's other great vocalist. You heard the steel band he loved so much playing her "E'oui sa vré" at every party.

Derek was a man of few words, of strong opinions and loyalties. He could be rough, and sentimental and chivalrous, and he knew how to laugh. One of my favorite pictures is of him bent over in hilarity with Roger Straus at FSG's fiftieth anniversary celebration. He loved being surrounded by those who he knew loved him and in his late years his birthday parties became ever more sizeable international gatherings.

Derek wasn't often open to suggestions. There was a tree in Castries near where we caught the catamaran for the birthday ride down the west coast to Ladera every January 23 that was always full of white egrets. A painting of it would have made the perfect jacket illustration for his last collection, but he never made it and the book appeared without an image.

No matter. His syllables are so mesmerizing because they are such a pitch-perfect transposition into language of what surrounds us, not the music of what happens so much as of what is always happening. His natural descriptions are full of metaphors of writing (and song) because that was what he was constantly doing, transforming what he saw and heard into lines that are perfect avatars of his world and, by extension, ours: of the world. When he left the beach the sea was still going on.

Never get used to this; the
　feathery, swaying casuarinas,
the morning silent light
　on shafts of bright grass,
the growing Aves of the ocean,
　the white lances of the marinas,
the surf fingering its beads, hail heron and
　gull full of grace,
since that is all you need to do now at your age
and its coming serene extinction like the light
　on the shale
at sunset, and your gift fading out of this page;
your soul travelled the one horizon, like a
　quiet snail,
infinity behind it, infinity ahead of it,
and all that it knew was this craft, all that
　it wanted —
what did it know of death? Only what you had
　read of it,
that it was like a flame blown out in a
　lowered lantern,
a night, but without these stars, the prickle of
　planets, lights
like a vast harbour, or devouring oblivion;
never get used to this, the great moon on these
　studded nights
that make the heart stagger; and the
　stirring lion
of the headland. This is why you have ended,
　to pass,
praising the feathery swaying of the casuarinas

and those shudderings of thanks, that so often
   descended,
the evening light in the shafts of feathery grass,
the lances fading, then the lights of the marinas,
the yachts studying their reflection in
   black glass.

PHOTOS OF DEREK

Derek with Roger Straus, care of Jonathan Galassi (Photo by Nancy Crampton)

Derek Walcott / Boston University / Thomas Sayers Ellis / 1989

Both of these photos are from rehearsals of *The Ghost Dance,* October 1989, taken at Slade Theatre, Hartwick College, Oneonta, NY, by Robert Bensen.

Above is Derek with the two actors, and below shows him with Sigrid Nama.

Derek Walcott and Joseph Brodsky, April 1980, at Trailways Bus Station, Oneonta, NY. Photos by Robert Bensen.

Galt McDermot, Bob Scanlan, and Derek Walcott during *Steel* production (1990)

Derek Walcott and Bob Scanlan 25 years after *Steel*

Derek with Seamus Heaney, care of Askold Melnyczuk (photo by Sigrid Nama)

John Robert Lee, Seamus Heaney, Kendel Hippolyte, Sigrid and Derek
Taken at Derek's house, circa 2008. Photo care of John Robert Lee

At the launch of Derek's *Morning, Paramin,* his last ever public reading
With Peter Doig, in St. Lucia, December 2016. Photo care of John Robert Lee

Two sketches of Derek
by artist Van Howell
Care of Eva Salzman

"Scotch, Right?"

Dan Hunter

"You? You wrote this?"

The words hung in the air, a cloud of disbelief laced with arrows of accusation. They were the first words that Derek Walcott ever spoke to me. My first inclination was to apologize and catch the first train back to Iowa.

Derek devoted the next two hours to ripping apart my play—the first page of the play. He also found time to denounce my sport coat as unfit for the theater. Derek positioned and repositioned the actors—who had never seen the script. He had them run the first page over and over again. If we made it to the second page, I was too stunned to notice, too absorbed in my own sense of failure.

As class departed, Derek pulled me aside. He wanted to know where I was from and if I were a poet. On the T riding home, I realized that he spent two hours on my piece—at least the first two pages—because he liked it.

When I knew him best, he taught poetry and playwriting in the graduate creative writing program at Boston University.

Derek was a teacher, intimidating by design. He believed in an Old-World style of teaching: students gather to listen to the master, learn the traditions, and learn the poetic meters. He believed that poets should write for the theater, and that playwrights should study poetry. So, he opened up his classes to both. Poets were invited to the playwriting class, and playwrights were welcomed into the poetry class.

I started going to his poetry classes in the fall of 1997 and continued to do so for 5 years. I'd like to think we became friends, but I think I was more of an equerry who would laugh at his bad jokes.

Derek always made an entrance into the poetry seminar room—stern, foreboding with measured strides. I once spotted him pausing before entering a playwriting class girding his loins. He seemed to be practicing his steely gaze:

"You? You wrote this?"

He rarely engaged in banter with the American students in his seminar. Although it was a creative writing class, we never heard or critiqued student poems. Instead, we read poems aloud sometimes solo, sometimes in unison. Poems by W. H. Auden, Hart Crane, Thomas Hardy, Delmore Schwartz, Emily Brontë, Philip Larkin and many others.

He expected us to memorize the poems for recitation in class. He loved to hear the poems out loud.

American creative writing classes typically function as a democracy where individual opinions are believed to carry equal weight. Students express their feelings good, bad, or indifferent. However, to Derek, the poems he chose for class were deeply moving and fascinating. The poems were almost like his children. They were to be studied, absorbed, revered, and remembered.

We were reading an Auden poem—a favorite of Derek's—when a student from California—wearing sandals in spite of the late fall chill—dribbled the classic whine: "well, it doesn't do much for me."

Derek was taken aback. "What do you mean?" After some back and forth, the student said, "well, it's not the way I would write it." Derek stood up and walked out. We waited. He didn't return.

So, I went to find Derek, outside in the cold, fuming. "Who does that asshole think he is? Auden? Nobody can be Auden."

Standing in the wind, we were silent for a few moments until he said, "You know where I live." Derek lived on the island of St. Lucia right on the water with a nightly view of the sun setting into the Caribbean. He had a beautiful house, a separate writing cabin, and endless warm weather. I understood that Derek was asking, "why do I put up with this?"

I don't know how long the class waited, but we went for lunch.

Derek didn't give up on students. He continued to teach at BU for six more years. He then taught at NYU. He was paid well for teaching. But I think he also felt a commitment to new writers. Derek had been the beneficiary of writers before him who handed down traditions, meters, and inspiration. I think he saw an obligation to pass down what he had learned.

And he invested in teaching writers. He used a portion of his MacArthur Foundation grant money to build the Boston Playwrights' Theatre at Boston University.

Derek was an intimidating teacher, seemingly aloof and intensely critical. He was difficult. He didn't want you to feel good. He wanted you to write well.

A student brought in a play to be read in class. The play is set in a working-class neighborhood bar in Gary, Indiana. It was a bar with regular clientele, a cadre of working men who drank together every night and had been for years. It is the night of a driving blizzard. Typically packed on a Friday night, the bar is completely empty except for the bartender. At first the bartender doesn't recognize the stranger who enters, brushing off snow. The stranger was formerly a bar regular that no one has seen for several years. The stranger had left factory work in Gary, for a high-paying job in Chicago.

What would the bartender say to a turncoat who escaped Gary, who probably thinks he's better than the regulars who stayed? Derek spent almost two hours on this question: how can you write dialogue that would convey the situation as clearly and succinctly as possible, that would capture the disdain the bartender felt?

It came down to two words: "Scotch, right?" The bartender greets him with "Scotch" to show he knows what his former customer used to drink. "Scotch" is followed by a cynical "right?" to ask, "or are you too good for us now?"

Finding the right words with the right rhythm is every writer's goal. Derek put all the possible variations of this scenario under the microscope. And when "Scotch, right?" emerged it instantly clicked into place. It was right.

I am deeply grateful not only for my friendship with Derek, but for his teaching. I see him in the front row of the theater turning around, pointing his finger at me, asking:

"You? You wrote this?"

AN EXCURSION &
AN INTRODUCTION

Karl Kirchwey

An Excursion: Derek Walcott at the
Mayflower Hotel (February 28, 1993)

I know I heard Derek Walcott read from his poems —perhaps his volumes Midsummer *or* The Arkansas Testament*—not long after I first started working at the Poetry Center of the 92nd Street Young Men's and Young Women's Hebrew Association in October of 1984. My first proper meeting with Derek, though, took place years later when I approached him about directing a New York reading of Seamus Heaney's version of Sophocles'* Philoctetes *called* The Cure At Troy *that was scheduled to take place in Kaufmann Hall at the Y on St. Patrick's Day of 1993.*

Derek had not only founded the Trinidad Theatre Workshop and the Playwrites' Theatre at Boston University, but had also written many plays (in verse and prose) of his own, including an adaptation of Homer entitled The Odyssey: a Stage Version *that would be presented in its turn at the Poetry Center.*

On a Sunday afternoon on the last day of February, then, I ventured over to the restaurant of the Mayflower Hotel on Central Park West. There I found the legendary publisher Roger Straus entertaining Joseph Brodsky, Seamus Heaney and Derek Walcott at brunch. Already a supplicant and considerably daunted by this company, I was given to understand that I could simply wait until they had time for me. Although this was long ago, no-smoking regulations were in effect in New York City restaurants. Derek insouciantly lit a cigarette. A waiter appeared and apologetically asked him to put it out. What happened next surprised me: Derek leaped up, as if to throttle the impertinent waiter, and was only barely dragged back into his seat by his poet-companions. In the many years since, I have had occasion to reflect on the contrast between the outward roughness and the interior gentleness of this poet.

There was to be a second meeting for me at the Mayflower with Derek Walcott, this one to discuss his directing of a reading of American poet Rita Dove's adaptation of Sophocles' Oedipus Rex *called* The Darker Face of the Earth, *scheduled to take place at the Y on November 20, 1995. Late in the afternoon of September 27 of that year, I arrived at the café of the hotel. Derek wanted me to eat something, so I ordered a slice of cheesecake and a cup of tea. He thought I should take advantage of the free crudités and dip, too. I sat directly across from him; he sat sideways in his seat and watched the large screen TV over the bar, which was filled with the faces of lawyers making statements as the jury was charged in the O.J. Simpson trial. At one point Derek looked at me and said, "You don't think you're more interesting than the O.J. trial, do you?" Such a remark was characteristic of a certain kind of masculine testing conducted by Derek. Every conversation with him began with a ritual exchange of insults (and it was important, I learned, to return the fire he directed at you); after this, one could move on to other things. But Derek's remark also revealed a restlessness of mind—the need to be thinking about more than one thing at once—that I understood was also characteristic of him. To his question I meekly replied, "Oh, no." Later Derek asked me, "Do you think he's guilty?" and I said "Yes I do." He replied, "I do too."*

We talked about casting for the Y reading. But then the Broadway producer Jimmy Nederlander strolled by on Central Park West, smiled, tapped on the café window and came inside to join us. Our meeting rather changed its focus as he and Derek began to discuss directors for the musical The Cape Man Derek was writing with his friend Paul Simon and the apartment on Central Park South Derek was to have for the month of November. Derek decided to move the meeting to another table in the café. Derek's companion Sigrid Nama arrived, and she and I had a chat. Jimmy Nederlander offered Derek and Sigrid tickets to a Broadway show on the weekend; further discussion followed. I left the Mayflower Hotel little wiser about plans for the reading of The Darker Face of the Earth than I had been when I arrived, but Derek did, in fact, agree to direct the reading.

The Rita Dove play is a kind of ante-bellum update in which Oedipus is an enslaved Black man and Jocasta (played in our reading by Barbara Feldon of sixties TV's Get Smart) a white plantation owner. Derek correctly remarked to the actors at the first rehearsal that the play is a melodrama, and then set about exploring ways to support the lines by means of the action onstage. The company included a number of wonderful young actors, and the energy and enthusiasm were running high. Derek had the company sing "Steal Away" and "My fader's done wid de trouble o' dis world," and worked in a passing over-and-under funeral ceremony. His resourcefulness and his ability to improvise, as a director, were wonderful to watch.

As the impresario, I was as usual involved in crazy last-minute missions: for $25, the Claremont Riding Academy (on the other side of Central Park from the Y) rented me a crop and a pair of spurs, and one hour before show time I found myself wandering up and down Park and Lexington Avenues looking for a pair of black shoes for Wendell Manwarren, an actor who had travelled to New York from the Caribbean to participate in the reading.

And now, looking back at my datebooks from so long ago, I see that I have placed the two meetings with Derek Walcott in a single venue, but in fact that winter brunch in 1993 took place at the popular Lincoln Center restaurant The Ginger Man, not at the Mayflower Hotel. And memory has also airbrushed out the presence of Derek's companion Sigrid Nama and Seamus Heaney's wife Marie at that first meeting, the better, I suppose, to highlight Roger Straus' remarkable triumvirate of male Nobel Laureate poets. A poet myself, could I belong, one day, to this brotherhood, in any way? Probably not; possibly so. I was never Derek's student, officially; but I had the privilege of working with him on bringing poetry to the stage, and my ideas about feeling, in lyric poetry, and about ambition, in narrative poetry, were indelibly marked by Derek's own work.

An Introduction: Derek Walcott at Bryn Mawr College (October 11, 2007)

Matthew Arnold's essay "The Study of Poetry" is famous because it was there that he formulated the dictum that poetry should be "a criticism of life." But also in that essay Arnold advanced his theory of poetic "touchstones," lines of poetry—by Homer, Dante, Shakespeare and Milton in particular—by which we can measure the "high and excellent seriousness" of all the poetry that comes after them. In his own essay "Making, Knowing, and Judging," W.H. Auden concludes that "…Arnold's notion of Touchstones by which to measure all poems has always struck me as a doubtful one, likely to turn readers into snobs and to ruin talented poets by tempting them to imitate what is beyond their powers." In our own age, of course, the notion of such "touchstones" is even more controversial.

One of Arnold's "touchstones" is a line from Dante's *Paradiso*, "In la sua volontade è nostra pace," "In His will is our peace," and notwithstanding Auden's skepticism, this line appears in Derek Walcott's recent long poem *The Prodigal*. But then, I am not sure that Mr. Walcott would disagree with Arnold's notion of "touchstones." I cannot say that Walcott has carried these "touchstones" like household gods on his back, fleeing a burning city to found a new empire across the sea, though there is always something of flight and distress in his work. He was, after all, *already* across that sea, at least half his ancestry carried there against its will. In an essay of 1970, Walcott wrote of his own poetic apprenticeship that "I saw myself legitimately prolonging the mighty line of Marlowe, of Milton, but my sense of inheritance was stronger because it came from estrangement." ("What the Twilight Says," 28)

Nonetheless, I think it is true to say that in Walcott's view, the poet cannot simply wish these "touchstones" away. In another essay, Walcott writes, "…while many critics of contemporary Commonwealth verse reject imitation, the basis of the tradition, for originality, the false basis of innovation, they represent eventually the old patronizing attitude adapted to contemporaneous politics, for their demand for naturalness, novelty, originality,

or truth is again based on preconceptions of behavior."
("The Muse of History," 54) Walcott is protective of the
intellectual and creative independence of the poet, and
contemptuous of what he refers to as "the poet as mass
thinker, as monosyllabic despot." Discovering a racial slur
in a letter of Robert Frost, a poet he reveres, Walcott is
disappointed but not surprised. And his conclusion is to
ask, "Now that other races and other causes in the babel
of the republic have been given permission to speak in
the very language that ruled and defined them, must
everything be revised by the new order?" ("Robert Frost,"
209). He answers that question with a warning: "...the new
order would be repeating the old order if it made a policy
of exclusion and an aesthetics of revenge."

Walcott once remarked of his friend and fellow-poet
Joseph Brodsky, "Such an intelligence needs bulk as much
as it needs particulars." And Walcott's own work has given
us both brilliant particulars and bulk. What *I* mean by
"bulk" is what used to be called poetic vision. For Walcott,
unusually in this era of the lyric poem, in book after book
insists on the largest narrative shapes for poetry. Walcott
writes *big* books. He speaks of "the weight, the slough,
the steady heave and lumbering movement in Brodsky's
hugely-designed poems," and once again this is an excellent
summary of Walcott's own poetic achievement.

"A great poem," Walcott has written, "is a state of
raceless, sexless, timeless grace." He has pursued his large
poetic shapes quite indifferent to the fads and orthodoxies
of the time in which he lives. He has never spared himself
the necessity of great art, wherever it may come from.

The Capitol of English Poetry

Adam Kirsch

Every poet begins as a provincial, dreaming of emigration to the city of the honored dead. "I think I shall be among the English poets after I die," wrote Keats, and the ambiguity is moving: he wants to be remembered as one of them, but also to actually walk and talk with them, like Dante with Virgil. To be born far from the center of literary society may, then, be an advantage to a poet's literary culture. He sees no reason not to converse directly with the authors he knows only from books; he does not need his passport

stamped by London or New York. This is the freedom that
allowed Keats, the Cockney poet, to be the direct heir of
Shakespeare; and it is the same freedom that drove Derek
Walcott, as a child on St. Lucia, to envy a blind neighbor,
thinking of "Homer and Milton in their owl-blind towers."
Today, after decades of writing some of the most beautiful
poems in the language, it is clear that wherever Walcott is,
there is the capital of English poetry.

SEEING WITH WALCOTT

John Robert Lee

I have often said that Derek Walcott helped me to see: my island, its land and sea-scapes, fauna and flora, as well as foreign cities and the painful heritages of history. Edward Baugh, in the introduction to his *Selected Poems of Walcott* (Farrar, Straus and Giroux, 2007) captures the comprehensive portrayal by the writer of his part of the world: "His evocation of the sensuous experience of the Caribbean, the modulations of Caribbean light... the changes of the Caribbean sea, generates images for apprehending Caribbean experience, for dealing with the pain of history and the colonial legacy of the region, its cultural palimpsest and mosaic." This was his contribution to international literature, this bringing of the multi-racial, multi-cultural, multi-lingual island archipelago into view. In well-formed lyric, descriptive-narrative sequences, and chapters of book-length poems, through his distinctive voice and with dramatic quality, he enabled readers everywhere to perceive, to see.

Morning, Paramin (Faber, 2016) was Walcott's final book, a sequence of short ekphrastic poems written in response to the paintings of Peter Doig. In his last two major works before this, *The Prodigal* (FSG, 2004) and *White Egrets* (FSG, 2010), the Nobel laureate leads us in looking with him, arguably more than before, and uniquely, at the inner regions of aging, death of friends, premonitions of his passing (which happened in 2017); there are reflections on fame and acclaim, his sense of declining gifts; old Europe and its history are recalled through travels in modern Europe and his growing love for Italy and Spain; and we feel with him his palpable relief in being home, at the end of fortunate traveling, in his beloved island of Saint Lucia. These two books read like confessional diaries, startlingly honest, in which he probes end-of-life observations, his metaphors as challenging as ever. We experience with Walcott these new regions of disturbing speculation. Given their several common themes they form companion late-life volumes.

A self-searching probing is heard in the voice of the prodigal persona: "Prodigal, what were your wanderings about?" (p. 70). This is the central question of the long poem. And in a deep irony, tied to his questioning in both books of fame and acclamation, we hear "approbation had made me an exile." (p. 79).

The probing, self-examination is also seen in the figure of the white egret, a symbol of poetics as well as a harbinger of death: "learn how the bright lawn puts up no defences/ against the egret's stabbing questions and the night's answer"; "they shall/ be there after my shadow passes with all its sins/into a green thicket of oblivion;" (p.6). In the last section of the title poem, his friend Joseph Brodsky is evoked (as he will be in *The Prodigal*) where a huge bird appears, "a sepulchral egret or heron," "perhaps the same one that took him." (p.10).

This aging prodigal with "desire and disease commingling" (p.7), describing himself as 'a spiritual lout" offers the first critique of his new work, "it's an old man's book/whenever you write it, whenever it comes out," (p. 8). And this challenge: "In what will be your last book make each place/as if it had just been made, already old,/ but new again from naming it." (p. 99).

He does not spare himself: "Threescore and ten plus one past our allotment,/in the morning mirror, the disassembled man." (p.53). And, "here is an old man standing in the door glass there,/silent beyond raging, beyond bafflement,/past faith, whose knees easily buckle."

The Sicilian Suite sequence in *White Egrets* takes a scalpel to age, infatuation and unrequited desire. "There was no 'affair,' it was all one-sided"; "he was the stubborn sacrificial victim/of his own hopes." (p.18).

If we see age through the eyes of this sensitive poet, both *The Prodigal* and *White Egrets* confront death through his record of the passing of loved friends, actors, writers and his twin brother. Though gone, they are still a presence. "I open their books and see their distant shapes/approaching and always arriving," (Egrets, p.12). *The Prodigal* memorializes Roderick Walcott, and Joseph Brodsky haunts both books. Inevitably, Walcott muses on his own death. If he will say he is "past faith", he can also still hope in the *White Egrets* for "that peace/beyond desires and beyond regrets,/at which I may arrive eventually." (p. 6). Death is expected, "everyone knows it will happen one day," (p.54).

While his vocation as writer always remains central, Walcott's historical ties to Europe shades these late books as much as his dead friends. Even as he records love for Italy and Spain he raises spectres of the old empires, their nagging prejudices, their monuments, their "chasm-deep surrendering of power" (Egrets, p. 36). His love for Europe's art and literature remains strong. And yet, the tensions of these two books, the life of the prodigal, a fortunate traveller, enjoying approbation with a certain caution, and the elusive egret teaching image selection, always spark forth: "After the museums and the sunlit streets,/… and the excessive solicitude of the concierge, /in all that completion there is still an emptiness." (Prodigal, p. 33). There is a deep querying for what truly satisfies this restless soul.

If Walcott had always felt himself an exile in Europe or America because of his race and colonial history, he says something additional in *The Prodigal* which he may not have voiced as clearly before: "Despite acclamation, despite contempt,/I was never part of that catalogue/in spite of friends in the same business/neither of the free-verse orthodoxy, nor the other —…Gradually it hardens, the death-mask of Fame." (p. 84). Aging seems to have brought its own doubts about his talent. In Egrets he writes with some despair: "…If it is true/that my gift has withered, that there's little left of it,/if this man is right then there's nothing else to do/but abandon poetry.." (p. 63).

In both of these final books, Walcott celebrates a return to St. Lucia where his last days were spent. In the major autobiographical *Another Life* (1973) he records how he and lifelong friend, the Saint Lucian painter Dunstan St. Omer

(1927-2015) had sworn that they would "put down, in paint, in words, / as palmists learn the network of a hand, / all of its sunken, leaf-choked ravines, / every neglected, self-pitying inlet..." They both kept their words, St. Omer became the leading painter of his generation, famous for his huge church murals that depicted the island and its people. All of Walcott's work, even as it traveled through the Caribbean and the world, always returned to Saint Lucia.

Mourning the death of his twin brother Roderick, he echoes *Another Life* in a chapter in *The Prodigal* that raises childhood memories and describes the island's beauty: "What was our war, veteran of threescore years and ten? / To save the salt light of the island / to protect and exalt its small people" (p.51). Enjoying the serenity of home, appreciating its beauty more deeply, he makes parallels between Europe and the Caribbean: "Both worlds are welded, they were seamed by delight." (p.71). Meditating on his travels through Europe, remembering the colonial history, we see Walcott claiming afresh, with a fierce joy, his island: "Do not diminish in my memory / villages of absolutely no importance, / the rattling bridge over the stone-bright river, / ...Hoard, cherish / your negligible existence, your unrecorded history / of unambitious syntax.." (p. 78).

Both books move to the peace of a prodigal's return, a gratitude that he has survived the vagaries of international applause. In *White Egrets*, he muses: "Wake up again to a dawn trembling with joy, / the silver beads on a dasheen leaf;.. / Cherish the uninterpreted light / of approaching eighty." (p. 68).

The Prodigal ends with an epiphany. He is on a boat and dolphins appear. It is a moment of resolution, even in the face of age, the scars of old battles, the certainty of death: "And always certainly, steadily, on the bright rim / of the world, getting no nearer or nearer, the more / the bow's wedge shuddered towards it, prodigal, / that line of light that shines from the other shore." (p. 105). And while *White Egrets* will cry out "So much to do still, all of it praise" (p. 83), it too will end near "the grooved sea / and the whole self-naming island, its ochre verges / its shadow-plunged valleys and a coiled road / threading the fishing villages, the white, silent surges / of combers along the coast." (p. 86). All ends where this modern master had begun at 18, and appropriately, "the book comes to a close." (p.86).

So, I have learned from Walcott, not only the passionate enthusiasm of visionary youth, the fervent love of writing and literature, the metaphysics of metaphor, the subtle battles that face us who come from small post-colonial societies, the desire for approbation, but with these two major final works, I have also observed the pilgrimages of prodigals through wildernesses of aging, death, the treacherous vanity fairs. He has enabled us to see the fundamental issues below the hurly-burly of our ambitions and achievements. And with him I have also seen that it is possible to return to blue-smoke valleys, egrets on the lawns, "the grooved sea" and the peace that only home can give.

CAZ AND GLYN'S
CHAT ABOUT DEREK

Caryl Phillips & Glyn Maxwell

By Email, 29 March - 14 April, 2022

CP: When did you first meet Derek?

GM: One sunny morning at BU's writing department, September 1987. He made fun of me being a Brit—which he never stopped doing—he seemed to like having one protegé each from as many countries as possible, so he could widely deploy cheap nationality jokes. But I knew he saw promise in my work, as he'd pushed for me to have a scholarship. This meant I was fairly relaxed when I met him. I didn't mind him making fun or—one time literally—ripping up a poem I showed him. I knew I was shallow and lazy, but I was where I wanted to be, with whom I wanted to learn from. He was politer to you, no? You were never his student!

CP: Well, I was never his student, but I think I also met Derek in 1987. He had a play on at Riverside Studios in London (it may have been 'O Babylon') and a producer friend of mine suggested he meet me for lunch in Shepherds Bush. I had just reviewed 'The Arkansas Testament' for the Los Angeles Times. Very positively! Anyhow, Derek was polite for about a nano-second, and then looked at the restaurant and said, 'An Indian restaurant! For lunch? Are you crazy?' Was he politer to me? I think because I had already been published by FSG, and had reviewed his work, he went a little easier on me than he did with you. But there was no such thing as a free ride. I think of you as not only a great writer, but a tremendously generous teacher and mentor. Do you think you got this from Derek because, as we both know, Derek loved to talk with younger writers.

GM: Simple answer: three sons with teachers for mothers! So I wonder if we all grew up with the instinct that the way towards the light was a loving figure knowing more than we did—which meant the way towards the light was also knowing we knew nothing yet. We could be mischievous or arrogant or lazy but we did know this. I definitely had it arriving at BU. As far as I was concerned, the metaphor for me was Derek at a pulpit and me sitting on the floor. The American way—I know he felt this—was chairs in a circle and everyone equal. I think that's why we got along so well. I would play the jumped-up new kid on the block but I was genuinely humble in the face of who he was and what he knew. Now he's gone and we're old bastards so it works the other way. We don't do chairs in a circle but I think we love the ones who care. And btw you're a great writer, teacher and mentor too, amigo, but you're definitely scarier to your students. I'm still working on that.

CP: Yes, it's good to be reminded that we're now the 'old bastards'. I like your distinguishing 'the ones who care'. It's true. Derek didn't like those who he thought were phonies or fakes. Either among his students or his peers. But he did like celebrity, didn't he? I suppose it was quite interesting for those of us as bystanders looking on; figuring out at what point celebrity met the world of 'fake', and wondering what exactly Derek was seeing and how he was navigating it all. At times, I could see it was a bit of a struggle for Derek, but one of the many things I learned from Derek was the reality of this particular dilemma, in the classroom and beyond. We have to constantly figure out 'the ones who care' from the ones who simply want to be seen and heard, but who perhaps have nothing to say beyond, 'look at me'. The truth is, Derek was generous enough—to both of us—to let us get close enough to him so we could occasionally witness him tussling with this aspect of being a writer and teacher.

GM: Certain things puzzled me at the time; they become clearer as I see more of his life in the round. It made no sense why—post-Nobel—he tried to get that Oxford Professor job. He *hated* writing prose essays. Any time he agreed to do one, he'd put it off for weeks and then turn into this big kid facing an all-nighter at school, saying he'd never write prose again. Also by that time he wasn't even *up* to flying to the UK three times a year for the length of the appointment. There was unfinished business with England, right? A complicated relationship, anyway. Some old scholarship? V S Nightfall? Can't remember. On the subject of celebrity nonsense, I also remember the day in 2011 when he won the T. S. Eliot Prize for *White Egrets*: it was in January so we were all at his place in St Lucia for the birthday week. English papers and TV stations kept phoning up the villa, looking for bullshit angles—things like 'So how's it feel to put one over on Heaney?' (who was shortlisted) and there they were, we could see them on the veranda, the best of friends, both delighted for him, going on with their breakfast. English rags, stay classy.

CP: Yes, the England thing was always complicated. For that generation of West Indian writer, the way out (and forward) was still the journey to England. As you know, Derek didn't get the scholarship to study at Oxford (like Naipaul), but he wasn't going to take his typewriter and jump on a ship as Selvon and Lamming did in 1950. He stayed and went to study in Jamaica, but I felt that he was always cognizant of the imagined 'authority' of England and English letters, while never being subservient to it. What do you think? I was teaching at Oxford when that Poetry Professor nonsense blew up and, like you, wished he'd never got involved. The *dramatis personae* lurking in the wings were toxic. However, I can't remember if you went to the Royal Shakespeare Company production of his stage version of 'Odyssey'. I travelled up to Stratford-upon-Avon with him (in 1993?) and it was a terrific day out. Despite a few crossed swords with the director, Greg Doran, Derek was in great form in the heart of England. After all, his father was called 'Warwick'. Why wouldn't he feel 'at home' in Warwickshire, right? But later, there was his teaching gig at the University of Essex, where you two were colleagues. How was he with England at this stage of his life? Was it pretty much just a job? Much like his subsequent gig in Edmonton, Canada? Or was there something else at play?

GM: Warwick! I never thought of that around those Stratford days. You're right about the England thing. Perhaps he'd have been happier if the place was *only* the literature. Some days I feel the same. It's sad to see it all draining away. Yes I went up to see 'Odyssey'—you and I didn't meet till the next year—and when I went there was this reading at the Swan Theatre. One time my students played the parlour game of 'Best Ever Poetry Reading', and I won with these cards: Derek, Heaney, Hughes, who introduced his poems with the words 'I've written some new poems about my first wife.' First time anyone heard any *Birthday Letters*. And Paul Simon was there, it was during Derek's *Capeman* Celebrity Years. Now I sound like an asshole namedropper too. Remember that running joke? Derek would tell us something about his new friend who once wrote *The Crucible* and married Marilyn Monroe and ask us in earnest 'You know Arthur?' So you and I would be, like, 'You know Tennessee?' 'You know Emily, Ann and Charlotte?' 'You know Percy Bysshe?' You have to seriously love someone to make fun like we did. I'm tearing up though, writing this. Essex was a beautiful brief shaft of light—Derek, Marina Warner, Wendell Manwaring coming to star in the plays, Maria Cristina Fumagalli, the stand-out Walcott scholar—that numbskull administration at Essex was so thick about what they had. When they regretted that they couldn't see their way to extending Derek's springtime visits, they acknowledged they'd been honoured to host the 'Noble [sic] Prize winner'. But I think he was delighted to see his old plays and new scripts getting done at Essex. He was ailing by then. But he made good friends, and at Edmonton too.

CP: Actually, that's what it was really about with Derek, wasn't it? The gift of friendship. The jobs—Boston, Essex, Edmonton, and other places too—were only important in terms of the friendships they produced. One of the joys of the last decade of his life was the annual gathering in St.Lucia for his birthday. It was there that we were able to see the evidence of his love of people. Each January, an eclectic, unpredictable, collection of people he had encountered on his travels descended on St.Lucia. Of course, as we both witnessed—many times—occasionally Derek's radar about people could be 'off'; Derek thought himself pretty vigilant about people's motives and, as a result, could be judgmentally 'firm' if he too sensed that something was 'off'. I don't know what you think, but I honestly felt that his temporary spasms of impatience would often come about because he so clearly wanted people to be the best they could be <u>and</u> to have *his* standards. Derek set the bar pretty high and didn't always understand when people couldn't measure up. But Derek's fundamental impulse was always to generosity, and I think we both loved him because of this. That said, when I look back now—with the benefit of hindsight—and think about some of the people who, over the years, crept into his world, I fully understand that Derek paid a price for his generosity. He bruised easily, didn't he? I think for many reasons. What do you think?

GM: Age, amigo, age. We witnessed some Lear-like moments towards the end, Act Three, mostly. But also, one of the last times we saw him, how he would get a literary thought in his head that he just *had to* communicate to someone who *had to know*. He kept summoning people into his room in St Lucia, asking them to find some passage of Hemingway—'do your internet thing', he would say—and the act of teaching transformed him to thirty years younger. Which is of course who he was when we met him. So it depended on what he was doing at any moment. Yes, he made some strange choices as time went on, but this is the only person I ever met, or will ever meet, who had—for better or worse—the psychological apparatus of kingship around him. You could walk with him in Derek Walcott Square in Castries, past a statue of Derek Walcott. It was his island. We saw that presentation one day at his restored childhood home, the Derek Walcott House, all the government officials there, where three young actors played Derek and his siblings as children. And there he was, watching from the front row. I remember thinking: did you want to live long enough to see your childhood acted out before you? Who knows. Those January trips were miraculous, really. Fortunate travellers, weren't we?

CP: Yes, we were extremely fortunate. And those years of 'kingship'—as you so aptly describe them—should they descend upon a writer, often turn that writer away from his or her desk and send them scuttling off in the direction of 'limelight'. Not so with Derek. His discipline was astounding and, of course, instructional. He served the word, and he inspired those around him with his enthusiasm for the word. In many ways, those St Lucia gatherings seemed to me to have been an opportunity for Derek to continue to 'teach' and have fun. After all, according to your own testimony, his method of teaching, while always rigorous, never excluded fun. Hardly a day goes by when I don't remember the example of Derek. Whether I'm at my desk, or in the classroom, I'm aware of his silent judgement.

However, there's no doubt that you were top of the class. You got his golden star, and 'Very Good' scrawled across the bottom of the final page. He described your book on teaching—*Drinks with Dead Poets: The Autumn Term*—as 'a masterpiece', and he meant it. Both your company and your work gave him pleasure, and I loved watching this unfold across three decades. Given the magnitude of the debt that we both owe him, it's nice to think that he may have got something from our loitering.

GM: Absolutely. Talking of *Drinks With Dead Poets*, one last anecdote. Yes he was very complimentary about the book, but he did tell me I 'hadn't quite got Byron right.' To which my only thought was 'How the fuck do *you* know?' Well maybe he does now. I hope we get *him* right too. Perhaps we made a start on that right here.

WORKING THROUGH OMEROS

Steven Ratiner

The worst crime is to leave a man's hands empty.
Men are born makers, with that primal simplicity
in every maker since Adam. This is pre-history,

that itching instinct in the criss-crossed net
of their palms, its wickerwork. They could not
stay idle too long. The chained wrists couldn't forget

the carver for whom antelopes leapt, or
the bow maker the shaft, or the armourer
his nail-studs, the shield held up to Hector

that was the hammerer's art. . .

— from Derek Walcott's *Omeros*

In 1990, when Derek Walcott's *Omeros* was first published, I was a forty-year-old poet trying to gain a small foothold in the literary world. I'd become the primary poetry reviewer for the *Christian Science Monitor* and so I quickly latched onto this title when it arrived—despite the challenge of coming to terms with an epic poem, over three hundred pages in length, in a matter of weeks. As I already admired Walcott's work, I thought writing about *Omeros* would simply be a labor of love. I underestimated the magnitude of the creation and thus the commensurate responsibility: to gain some substantial insight into what, it turned out, would come to be regarded as Walcott's magnum opus.

Taking an ancient text as a starting point (in this case, Homer's *Iliad*, with a little of the *Odyssey* and Dante's *Inferno* tossed in for good measure), Walcott fashioned a modern incarnation, this time featuring an all-Caribbean cast of characters. The poet's aim was to create a poem with tremendous resonance for his contemporary readers while offering us a fresh perspective on the enduring Homeric mythology. Of course Walcott's project bore a kinship to that of Joyce's *Ulysses* but, I see now, I focused perhaps too much on their shared technical prowess and not enough on the historical burden these writers were carrying. Walcott's poem is broken up into seven books (further divided into numerous chapters, each of which comprised of three cantos); with a loosely circular structure, we follow the conflict between Hector and Achille, fishermen from Walcott's native St. Lucia (all the characters bear Westernized names, mostly reflecting the Greek figures in its origin tale) as they wrestle with life in a poor postcolonial society and vie for the love of an ebony island beauty. Helen is the sort of woman who turns heads whenever she appears; but the attitude with which she carries herself (branded as *haughtiness* by the locals)—not to mention her refusal to submit to the advances of Western tourists—has left her unemployed and unencumbered. This metaphorical connection between the old and new worlds existed even outside of the poet's imagination: St. Lucia's old nickname was 'the Helen of the Caribbean' because it had been battled over so often by the British and the French—and so this idea must have been simmering in Walcott's unconsciousness for many years.

Through this poetic journey, the poet pays homage to, not one but two monumental sources: as a bow to Homer's creation, he continually plays off the *Iliad*'s narrative about the Trojan War in sly and unexpected ways, and tends to write in 12-syllable lines, a loose approximation of the Greek hexameters (though he often violates that stricture when it suits his purposes.) He also composes all the verse in the *terza rima* form meant to bring to mind those famed three-line stanzas of Dante's *Divine Comedy*; and because of its interlocking rhyme scheme, his tercets are woven together like an elaborate fishing net of narrative. In addition, Walcott brings to bear (as he does throughout his verse) lush imagery and startling metaphors, all shaped into incantatory lines—the sort of musical richness that was, even then, falling out of fashion, but which I found deeply satisfying. In short: this was a masterwork. Two years later, Walcott would be awarded the Nobel Prize for Poetry, and most agreed that *Omeros* was the tipping point.

By temperament, I was always the reclusive sort—and so I never took full advantage of Walcott's years teaching in the Boston area. I attended readings and exchanged a few words at receptions, but refrained from approaching this poet in any meaningful way—that is, until the close of 1999 when I created a sprawling art project for First Night's Millennium Celebration. Bringing together several dozen poets, musicians, dancers and visual artists, *Big Night in the Book House* was designed to fill the main branch of the Boston Public Library with a confluence of artforms. Knowing, though, that neither budget nor circumstance would allow me to include the voices of some of our area's signature poetic talents, I decided to add a video component to the program. Working with a crew of Boston University Film and Video students, I set out to make four elaborate poetry videos, each recorded at the homes or workspaces of the participating poets, which would then premier at the New Year's Eve event. My plan was to feature one poem each from Mary Oliver, Donald Hall, Frank Bidart (most of whom I knew from an interview series I wrote for the Monitor), plus Derek Walcott who was essentially a stranger.

I must have written a convincing letter because Walcott agreed…then withdrew…then signed on again as, week by week, I'd beseech him in phone calls to New York City trying to nail down arrangements. Elusive and protective of his privacy, the poet also seemed offended that I wasn't offering him at least some payment for his performance— and, looking back, I can see now that this displayed a certain naïveté for a fifty-year-old who was shepherding such an ambitious project. I couldn't imagine that money would be a concern to a Nobel Prize winner; more than that, I hadn't given enough thought to the symbolic nature of *payment*, how we honor what we value. Since my budget was already overcommitted, I offered to pay him a hundred-dollar honorarium from my own pocket (something I could ill-afford at the time.) No, the poet explained gently, the money had to come from the arts organization; it was a matter of respect. After a flurry of phone calls, I told him I'd been able to secure the honorarium—though, in truth, I simply fronted the money, desperate for my representation of Boston-area poetry to include the Nobel Laureate as its crowning jewel.

The video was to be shot on the stage of the Playwright's Theater which Walcott founded. I explained my plan to couple the poet's reading of "Thanksgiving" (a poem set in both his native St. Lucia and adoptive Boston) with a musical performance by Bala Tounkara, a *griot* and *kora* master from Mali, West Africa who I'd recently met. I didn't recognize until I began writing this very essay—two decades later—how the suggestion of that pairing was probably what convinced Walcott to take part in my production, for reasons I was incapable of fathoming at the time.

Fast forward to 2022: having been invited to contribute to this all-Walcott issue, I mentioned my old review of *Omeros* to Arrowsmith's editor; he quickly encouraged me to write something centered on that text. Of course I agreed but, I confess, quivered again to realize how much work I'd just made for myself: re-reading the massive poem; examining some of the wealth of critical writing that's been done about it; and, I quickly understood, confronting in my present self the shadow of the younger.

I began considering exactly what was the nature of this literary work and the source of its power. As a young poet, I was drawn to the sheer bravado of such an undertaking, and imagined that Walcott had something he needed to prove, to earn the fullest respect from the literary and academic worlds. Presumptuous as it sounds, I've always sensed a childhood brokenness inside this poet, despite his outward panache and self-assuredness—though, of course, this doesn't require some uncanny psychological deduction. I believe we all carry within us a place where we were broken by the world—wounded by some early disappointment in who and what we most needed in our lives. The more I thought about this text, and the more I explored Walcott's background, I realized how limited my perspective had been. How could I possibly comprehend the damage to a young person's sense of self, growing up in a climate of historical, political and cultural subjugation? I've heard tales—concerning Walcott and other Caribbean writers—about the desire to excel that sometimes arises under such a system, to prove one's worth (or, at the least, to disprove the low expectations a white British educational system maintained for the young Black students in its classrooms.) 'Postcolonial literature'—and *Omeros* became one of the prominent subjects for study—has generated something of an academic cottage industry. Central in discussions was the concept of the two main paths open to the creative mind: assimilation (proving yourself a better and more literate Englishman, for example, than the ones instructing you); and rebellion, often retreating into a defensive posture, focused perhaps on indigenous mythology and local dialect. But more recently, a third middle ground has been described—a *hybrid imagination*, as it's called—that tries to fashion a new path from this blending of cultures.

In *A Companion to Twentieth-Century Poetry*, Bruce Woodcock wrote the chapter on Walcott's *Omeros*. He draws on an idea Salman Rushdie put forth in his essay "Imaginary Homelands": that both the postcolonial writer and subject matter revolve around a 'translated' existence. "[Rushdie] points out that the word 'translation' is derived from the Latin for 'bearing across': 'Having been borne across the world, we are translated men. It is normally supposed that something always gets lost in translation; I cling, obstinately, to the notion that something can also be gained.'" Woodcock continues: "Walcott is well aware of the contradictory legacies of such translations. Hence, *Omeros* is a work which, rather than translating Homer, translates Walcott's home island of St. Lucia into the epic dimension of the Homeric form; but at the same time, it interrogates the notion of such translations, and asserts the actuality of the lived experience of the island, outside the artificial confines of literature and art. It aims to heal the cultural schizophrenia of a hybrid history and the translations of the colonial process."

Omeros begins with a scene that almost amounts to a temple desecration: Philoctete, a wounded fisherman, is making a little extra money by offering guided tours to vacationers. He's reciting the story of how the fisherman, wielding axes, cut down the old cedars to make their *pirogues*, dug-out fishing canoes. Immediately the narrative takes on mythic proportions. The men he depicts are caught between the vestiges of their old forest gods and the exigencies of the modern world where the sea, for the most part, is their only source of livelihood. Speaking in a Caribbean patois (something Walcott largely avoided in the past), the fisherman says:

"Wind lift the ferns. They sound like the sea that feed us
fishermen all our life, and the ferns nodded 'Yes,
the trees have to die.' So, fists jam in our jacket,

cause the heights was cold and our breath making feathers
like the mist, we pass the rum. When it came back, it
give us the spirit to turn into murderers."

It was the first of many passages threading through *Omeros* about the nature of and the necessity for work—how lives are shaped by their commitment or servitude to certain labors. It may be surprising at first, but we quickly accommodate ourselves to Walcott's startling venture: why *shouldn't* these 'small' lives be depicted in monumental terms since they are integral in this magnificent landscape, and take place beneath these majestic skies? "These were their pillars that fell, leaving a blue space/ for a single God where the old gods stood before." In *Omeros*, all the island feels like a spiritual text that must be interpreted: by Hector and Achille, in their struggles to compete and survive; by Ma Killman who sells Coca Cola and sundries in her No Pain Café (but who also exchanges her 'church clothes' for traditional dress and assumes the role of *obeah* to reclaim the ancient island language, communicate with the dead, and work traditional cures); and even by Sergeant Major Plunkett and his wife Maud, British expats who have also been wounded by history and have sought renewal in St. Lucia. I mustn't overlook the weary old spirit referred to, alternately, as Seven Seas or Omeros, who helps guide our progress; and, even more surprising, another 'I' narrator who seems to be Walcott himself, returned to his island home to come to terms with the burden of his own troubled memory.

This morning, a sudden recollection from, of all places, high school science class. I remember being taught that, in physics, 'work' is computed by a simple formula: force times *displacement*—how much force is exerted to move what mass over what distance. Revisiting Walcott's text, three decades later, this seemed less like a *tour de force*—the sort of thing meant to impress critics—than an utterly necessary act of self-preservation. Approaching sixty at the time, Walcott was keenly aware of the conflicting forces within his own career (within his very identity). Once this poem began to unscroll its narrative possibilities, I believe he accepted it as work long-postponed: confronting the variety of displacements he'd experienced since childhood, and the winding journey that had brought him to his present circumstance. Shaping such a work, marshalling the force to attain a new awareness—this might be the sort of act that rescues heroes, reclaims the idea of *home*.

In his essay "The Wound of History: Walcott's *Omeros* and the Postcolonial Poetics of Affliction" Jahan Ramazani writes: "Early on in *Omeros*, Walcott uses one of Philoctete's seizures to suggest that the inexpressible physical suffering of enslaved Africans is retained in the bodies of their descendants and that the pain still presses urgently for an impossible verbal release." Though the history of slavery and colonization might not arise in everyday thought, it's hold upon memory and even the body cannot be overlooked. But doesn't this hint at the work every individual must take responsibility for: to identify the immense cargo our consciousness, by its very nature, cannot help but transport—the personal, familial, and historical? And then comes the real labor: to celebrate what we are able—and make at least an attempt to heal the suffering we uncover, our own as well as those around us. I recalled poet Jane Hirshfield's marvelous essay collection *Nine Gates*. In the piece entitled "Poetry as a Vessel for Remembrance", she writes movingly about the power of memory and song, central in the Homeric creation, stemming from a time before the invention of books eroded the mesmerizing hold

of the oral tradition. She describes that "immense shadow…
[that] lives on in virtually every characteristic by which
we recognize poetry"; and she makes the claim: "This,
then, is the world of Mnemosyne, in which all knowledge
has been hard won, braced against the erasures of time
by generations of singers and their words…It is a mind in
which knowledge is embedded in the recital of outward
description and actions, and in which new information
immediately becomes the basis for a new story." This,
certainly, describes the particular muse who moved in with
Walcott in his St. Lucia home, placed this new task upon
his opened notebook, and required of him a more sustained
and sustaining song.

In interviews, Walcott resisted the classification 'epic'
for *Omeros* because his poem lacked a single protagonist
wrestling with what seems to be an overarching fate. In
fact, canto by canto, the reader swims in and out of all
his characters' minds, steered by their diverse narrating
voices. So I've come to regard this book in the way Freudian
analysis confronts dreams: the poet is *all* of these characters,
is embodied in every element including the land- and
seascape itself. The protagonist is the human mind that
can contain all this vision, remember all this song. I was
delighted when I came across a recording of a 2008 BBC
podcast of *World Book Club* where the poet sat for questions
about *Omeros*. He spoke of its origin in writing a single
piece focusing on the character Philoctetes, "and I don't
quite know when the line came that said *this was a beginning*
but when it came… it was in the pitch of the St. Lucian
fisherman's voice." He speaks of the compulsion that drove
him onward as "a liberation." "And I said [to myself]: I

don't care if this poem is liked or read or popular—and I felt a total freedom" from the strictures all published writers must contend with: career and audience. "I looked forward—once the form [of the book] was established, and the momentum of the form was there. It must be the same pleasure that a novelist has in writing a book, that you get up in the morning and you know you have to do chapter six, and your work is there for you, so you have a job. . .it was exhilarating to work on it."

Walcott was making "a poem about associations not derivations"—not a Caribbean dependence upon the Western canon, but the way every consciousness, in any one moment, draws upon the totality of their experience, bringing to it a unique set of interrelated impressions. In that case, I would say that this long poem—epic in scale if not by strict definition—was fashioned to be a neural matrix of the poet's associative connections: to St. Lucia and the history of his people; to the long and complex poetic tradition he's inherited; to his own memory storehouse, both painful and glorious; and the urge (individual and societal) for the dispossessed to *repossess* their geographical/spiritual home via an act of the imagination. There is an evolution most poets undergo: from writing *poems* to writing *poetry*; at the conclusion of his sixth decade, this poet was bringing to bear the skill and intuition developed from forty-plus years of his writing practice in order to simply immerse himself in this unfolding narrative—I should say, *skein* of narratives. Its purpose: that the weight of an emotional displacement he'd experienced all his life might be transformed, transported, and set down into some new circumstance. It was necessary work for the poet—and, because of his prodigious talent and imaginative breadth, it was work we could participate in for three hundred pages before, exiting the poem, we'd find our hands and hearts at work on our own long-postponed labors.

Derek Walcott sat perched on a stool on the darkened stage of the theater that was, in part, his spiritual home—and the warm spotlights washed across the side of his face, his hunched over body. He read slowly and carefully allowing the articulate music of syllables to guide him. Across the stage, Bala Tounkara sat with the *kora's* calabash gourd in his lap, thumbs plucking the strings rising along the hardwood neck. I sat directly in front of the poet and served as his solitary audience, an incalculable delight. After the recording was finished, I sat with Walcott and—relaxed now, his theatrical responsibilities complete—he spoke with me about poetry, St. Lucia, his feeling for his own African roots. I could sense the vulnerability at the heart of his complex imaginative life. And I saw more clearly that there was a certain privilege involved—a matter of race or background, I wasn't sure—in my earlier misapprehension of poet and poem. How could I have supposed that the award of a Nobel Prize would also serve as a shield from the world's slings and arrows, or armor any man against the internal doubts and fears by which memory and legacy sometimes target us? Before we parted ways, Walcott signed my copy of *The Bounty*, the collection that contained the poem we'd just recorded. I also presented him with his hundred-dollar honorarium.

The check was never cashed.

Fancy the Flight

Eva Salzman

The last time I was supposed to see Derek Walcott was at Goldsmiths—University of London where I teach part-time. Discovering he was visiting England, I'd nabbed him for a reading at the college, and then got sick on the appointed day.

Derek read from *White Egrets*, his poetic memoir about coming to terms with old age, aging and death, including the aging and death of lovers—among the more moving poems in the book I thought—with these topics accompanied by varying (r)egrets. My artist ex-husband attended, taking notes and dashing off a few drawings of the man. Reports from students describe a fantastic reading, and Derek as personable and generous during the Question and Answer.

A painter too, Derek shared his belief that poets should do more than one thing. As an ex-dancer who plays pool and likes to shoot a gun—an admission one shouldn't share with liberal friends—I concur, also relating to his rapport with the pen as the instrument best suited for composing poetry. Writing, he thought, has a relationship with the body. (An essay I wrote for the UK journal Poetry Review, "Dance and Metaphor", touched on the crossroads between the visceral, intellectual and poetic.) One attendee called the discussion after the reading 'unusual', perhaps not appreciating the dark humor of Derek's solution to a student's asking advice about writer's block:

'Suicide', he'd replied.

I don't recall what my illness was but I felt sicker—and surprised—when hearing that Derek had been annoyed at my absence. After all, the event was well-attended and well-received, and I'd met him only once in Brighton (UK), many years after studying with him at Columbia University's MFA program when I wasn't aware of appearing on his radar at all. I was somewhat nervous chatting after his Brighton Festival reading, for good reason. When my father had been Artistic Director of the American Music Theater Festival in Philadelphia, Derek had been fired from the role of Director of his own piece. My father saying this in a light jokey tone suggested an anecdote niftily honed into hyperbole. Good lord, I thought. How unthinkable. It's possible what actually occurred was nothing more than a difference of opinion followed by a mutually agreed outcome.

My notes and recollections on this matter pertain to a piece called *Capeman* which my father and/or others hadn't thought was a good idea in the first place, especially after it became a multimillion-dollar extravaganza into which the singer/songwriter Paul Simon had poured half his fortune. A top-name's considerable financial expense on an impending disaster was front-page news, apparently, although my notes don't specify which front page. It seems that the previous Director had resigned a performance thought doomed and when Derek stepped in to replace him, an already bad production became even worse. It may be the case that nobody could have saved it by then. Mark Morris as choreographer added another name to a stellar line-up one might think would guarantee success. These facts, derived from old notes and patchy recollections, may not be facts at all, but are perhaps enough to cause anxiety in Brighton, and later in London too.

Needless to say, I steered clear of mentioning my father in Brighton, or any subjects that could lead in that direction. The issue never arose, and no grudge or anger was evident. The exchange was civil, and fun. Either he didn't blame me or couldn't have cared less or failed to recall the incident or just didn't know that I knew. Maybe he hadn't even connected the Salzman dots.

Still, at the Goldsmiths reading, Derek's view was that illness was no excuse for missing it. This expectation's tinge of entitlement may partly account for a degree of ambivalence I feel towards a poet who was nevertheless one of my most influential and memorable writing teachers. His seating us in an empty theater for lessons on poetry as a spoken performative art made perfect sense; even if I hadn't come from a musical performative background, it was just plain exciting.

So I felt sicker still when the Goldsmiths event turned out to be the last opportunity to ever see him again. And I feel sickest of all now, admitting to myself and to this page, a nagging suspicion that my body conspired with a subconscious wish not to attend the reading at all.

I can only speculate about my own subconscious, but such speculation happens to be a favorite hobby. It may have been a fit of pique over Goldsmiths' endemic shoddy treatment of faculty. Then there was the daunting unforgettable experience of Columbia's MFA program, compounded by other insecurities. Many fellow students were older than I was, certainly more adult and mature. They'd been published, had had jobs, even been married and had lived out in the wide world. At least one had observed illness and death up close. In contrast, I'd sprung fresh and green straight from Camp Bennington, as my undergraduate college was sometimes jokingly called, a designation a bit unfair to those of us not from rich families who could attend only thanks to substantial scholarships.

The first day I stepped into Derek's classroom I found him intimidating; I believe anyone would have objectively found him so. His teaching was adversarial in style, on-the-spot writing assignments issued as imperatives and challenges. He and Joseph Brodsky, with whom I also studied at Columbia, made a formidable team within a formidable program. Further context amplifies this formidability. New York City itself was a radically different environment then, at the tail-end of being the quintessential New York City (to some): meaning dirty, dangerous but exciting too.

At the same time, in America generally, the prevalent poetry aesthetics were antagonistic to craft and fusty metricists. Using rhyme almost felt like a failure to show respect for or proper allegiance to the culture. The challenges in a chaotic place were paradoxically paralleled in the classes of two poets for whom tradition was not merely important but essential. Derek and Brodsky's ostensibly outdated pedagogy and literary principles lay in a formal direction I was already headed, writing sonnets in secret behind the bike-shed. If your version of rebellion entailed traveling backwards in time and numerous demands, they were the teachers for you. I attended their classes religiously.

Sarah Arvio described their bromance, and their 'quipping and telling jokes with hand gestures'. She herself has called Derek 'wry and affable', concluding her remarks enigmatically by saying "many anecdotes that can't be told': which comment suggests she knew them much better than I did. While both were demanding, Derek struck me as more arbitrarily harsh in how he put students on the spot. Yet, this had a positive constructive effect too, likewise in tandem with the environment, helping to cultivate a drive to rise to the occasion and to the dynamic that prevailed in their classes, and countering the aforementioned insecurities.

Neither Derek nor Brodsky ever saw my writing since I studied literature with them. The ambivalence mentioned earlier might also be traced to being aware, in their classes especially, that woman students merited less attention. Later would come a fuller recognition of the preponderance of male authors generally on the American syllabus, from grade school all the way up to university. Later still came a fuller realization of what women writers had to contend with since most of the power was held by male editors and publishers.

It was impossible to be oblivious to the scandals associated with Derek within academia from which he seemed to emerge unscathed. In Brighton, I'd glimpsed this side of him, if briefly and mildly. There was a certain salaciousness in both his expression and the tone of his response to my mention of Bennington:

"Ah, a Bennington girl. Bennington...."

A book can own you, said Derek, and from my earliest memories literature had owned me. He and Brodsky were a two-pronged intellectual force drawing me in. Their vigor and rigor were necessities.

If we're going to call ourselves poets, Derek said, we should know the canon; if you say 'horse' you should be able to name any number of poems with a horse in them and know the lines. Derek's view of rhyme as a test of ability might seem to some unacceptably sportsmanlike, competitive and cold. Yet he also compared the perfect harmony of a rhyming couplet to two lovers. For him poetry is like prayer in its communion of spirit between writer and reader.

Derek has traced his own impetus to write to the age of one, and the death of his father, who wrote too. He wanted to continue his father's work. As it happens, his repeated references to birds rhyme with my childhood experience too, since my composer father was also a Long Island birding expert and mycologist of sorts: an artist who fulfilled Derek's proscription that writers—and thus, surely all artists—do more than one thing. Derek once described the albatross as a metaphor for poetry because it's ungainly before it takes off and *White Egrets*, his swan song, exemplifies this affinity with birds. He also said that poets' real biographies are 'like those of birds [because] their real data are in the way they sound."

Another quotation of his calls bad art prophetic, racial or nationalist; he adds that great art has moral power and is modulated by honesty. Earthy scandals within ivory towers, such as those associated with him, remind us what we already know—from reading the diaries of Woolf, Wagner and Larkin, for example—which is that we may love the art yet be uncomfortable with aspects of the artist. Derek's own poems and comments are those of an oracular poet aware of the limits of oratory, even as he himself earned passage into the pantheon of eminent literary statesmen.

Above all else, perhaps, Derek called poetry a consolation or else it wouldn't be created by people in great pain. When I reviewed *White Egrets* for Poetry London some years ago, I finished the piece as I'll finish here:

Although the powers on display here bode well for more to come, the collection hedges its bets finally with a majestic flourish, in commandingly lyrical style:

As a cloud slowly covers the page and it goes
White again and the book comes to a close.

GONE ASTRAY:
DEREK'S ECLIPSED MUSICAL, *STEEL*

Bob Scanlan

Derek approaching a microphone or a podium was a study in arrogant disdain, a *performance* of the subtext *"I'm not what you think... but something much above this trivial occasion."* His carriage, his fierce, unsmiling mien were always his opening gambit in live performances. But in a rehearsal hall—or inside his own Playwrights' Theatre at Boston University—Derek was a loose, funny, garrulous, charming and boyishly happy man. His smile and his laughter were infectious and seductive. We all had fun (sometimes too much) and learned and practiced our *theatre* craft in his company by osmosis and by contagion.

I mean here mainly to write about *Steel*, a forgotten major musical, with book and lyrics by Derek and a superlative score by Galt MacDermot—famous as the composer of *Hair*. I directed the world premiere of *Steel* at the American Repertory Theatre in 1991, a year before Walcott's Nobel Prize. *Steel*—book, lyrics and score—was left behind and never published or revived... probably because we all realized the book (especially the second act) was a mess in the form we had managed to give it. I regret to this day that we never recorded a cast album of Galt's blockbuster score. It would have placed a marker for *Steel* but the onrush of events buried that glorious but flawed work. And then, disastrously, Derek got embroiled in the gigantic, heavily publicized, Broadway boondoggle of *Capeman*. After wasting over twelve million dollars of Broadway investment capital, no musical by Derek could be so much as mentioned... ever again.

I was assigned to direct the new musical, but first it had to be written and composed. Galt MacDermot was Derek's choice (the two had worked together in 1974 on Walcott's play *O Babylon*, for which Galt wrote incidental music) and the ART was happy to commission the music from him. The ART then assembled a large and gifted team of collaborators: set and costume designers, lighting designers, choreographers, stage managers, dramaturgs, prop builders and assistants of all kinds. We embarked on the creation of *Steel*. We had to cast a large and almost all-black cast of good actors and better singers, we had to assemble a pit band that included expert steel pan players and—a great boon—Galt MacDermot agreed to the huge task of being not only the composer, but also our musical director for the whole production period. This included casting the singers after exhausting and protracted auditions in New York. It also included rehearsal accompaniment throughout the weeks prior to opening. Galt had to teach his own music, coach the singers and conduct the band while also playing a reduction of the score on the piano in endless rehearsals. This huge team process was to dominate the next two years of our lives, and Galt, Derek and I lived and breathed "*Steel*" 24/7 for many months together. It's hard to describe how well I got to know Derek Walcott during those intensely interactive two years: it seemed like all *Steel* all the time. We were together seemingly day and night, and we traveled together repeatedly, mainly back and forth to New York, where we stayed in the Gramercy Park Hotel. It was in the hotel's lobby that I first heard many of Galt's songs, sung raucously by Galt himself as he accompanied himself on the lounge piano. We caused a sensation at the hotel. And Derek drew the sincere attention of countless women once he was recognized....

Derek and Galt creating songs for *Steel* in 1990 (Photo Bob Scanlan)

Steel opened on April 3, 1991 at the Hasty Pudding Theater in Harvard Square, where it played to sold-out audiences for three weeks before transferring to Philadelphia for a second run at the American Music Theater Festival. It made good box office there, too, but it got slammed by all its critics in both cities. The score and the steel pan music were electrifying, but the book was—especially in the convoluted second act—all-but incomprehensible. No one could follow it to the end. I was forced, finally, just before we opened, to write an insert for the program summarizing the convoluted plot. Here is the crib sheet for the first act alone (which included, at one time 29 songs, of which 8 were eventually cut!)

Synopsis of Act I of *Steel*

The setting is Laventille Hill, behind the East Dry River bridge in Port of Spain, Trinidad. Growler, an old calypsonian past his prime, has been hopelessly in love with his next-door neighbor, Joyce Seedansingh, who became a prostitute after being abandoned by her U.S. Marine lover at the close of the Second World War. Joyce has sheltered her daughter by the American Marine (her name is Zora) in her home village of Tableland, but has now brought her daughter to the city to acquire the education she needs to start a life somewhere off the hill. Next door lives Winston Marshall, a good student who is being groomed by his religious foster parents (Uncle Daniel the tailor and Aunt Jessica) to compete for a scholarship to study at the London School of Music. Winston's teacher, Lawrence-Bain, has invested all his own ruined hopes of high cultural achievement in his star pupil. But young Winston is irresistibly attracted to the life of the panyard, where neighborhood toughs are creating a new identity and a new music based on the steel pan instrument invented and perfected by craftsmen like Eli Manette. These pans are dented ingeniously from abandoned (or stolen) industrial oil drums left behind by large American petroleum concerns like Texaco.

When the play begins, the captain of the Bandidos steel band (Bones) and one of the players (Roger "Reds" des Ruisseaux) take Winston along on a midnight raid of the Texaco storage yards, where they steal an empty oil barrel for Eli to fashion into a new "pan." In the course of this escapade, Roger stabs a policeman. A local Trinidad entrepreneur, Joseph Arenkinian (whose Syrian grandfather owns Laventille Hill) allies himself with a big American oil drilling firm and tries to contract the Bandidos to promote his business interests in New York. Exploiting Roger's legal difficulties, Arenkinian arranges his release in exchange for a cut-rate three-year promotional music contract which takes Roger and Winston to New York. Meanwhile, alarmed over her daughter Zora's infatuation with the disreputable panman Winston, Joyce strikes a bargain with her daughter: she will give up prostitution and return to Tableland if Zora agrees to give up Winston and leave Trinidad for better opportunities in America.

This first act —and its 21 musical numbers—might have been manageable by itself. But Derek could not be induced to temper his ambitions for a chaotic continuation into a second act, one with intricate plot twists, flashbacks, and new scenes now set in New York (his *Orpheus in Hell* passages) and elsewhere in new locations off Laventille Hill, our basic setting in the theatre. It included 17 more musical numbers, which Galt continued to compose gamely and unquestioningly, as Derek continued to churn out plot occasions and lyrics. Galt one day told me that Derek's lyrics instantly inspired him. "I don't know what it is about Derek's lyrics... but when I read them, I hear the music and just write it down." This led eventually to a grand total of some 40 Galt MacDermot songs. At the time I probably was (and may still be) the *only* person who had kept track of the *sequence* of the ever-growing score. I still hold notebooks full of "plot-bead diagrams" of the play, by means of which I tried to keep a grip on the plot structure. But here Derek's and my collaboration broke down: he would not let me "dramaturg" (trim, shape, cut, rearrange) the play—something all directors must be at liberty to do, especially with new work working its way through a first production. We arrived helter-skelter at the unavoidable pre-scheduled and pre-sold opening night.

We received endless kudos from audience members who had had a wildly good time at the theatre. But the critics were severe. A few of them acknowledged the crazy intoxication and the beauties of the score, but none could overlook the basically unfinished and confusing incoherence of the book.

This state of affairs was complicated by the fact that Galt and Derek's musical attracted a substantial new audience from the Black and Caribbean communities. Never had the ART or Harvard Square hosted such a largely black audience and they were attracted by the almost all-black cast, the Afro-colonial story, the exotic setting, the advertised steel-pan music (many members of our band had been recruited in Dorchester and Roxbury) and the fame of Derek Walcott. Our audiences loved us and gave us terrific "word-of-mouth" publicity and sales—the best way to fill a theatre. But we had also consumed inordinate amounts of production money—paying and housing a large and expensive cast, multiple paid "workshops" of the book and score before production, always *with* musicians (whose union rates break the bank in theatres), many extended trips to New York, and lavish sets and costumes. We did not break even, but we weren't a disaster—except critically.

My explanation for the devastating press reviews, which "killed" any future for the show—even then— was that we had just run out of time. Derek did not know how to untangle himself from the innumerable twists and turns of his novel-length plot. I did, but it involved cuts and amputations Derek was unwilling to make. I also had a devil of a time mediating between Derek, his titanic temper, and our disgusted Artistic Director, Robert Brustein, another titanic personality—who continually harangued me to get Walcott to accept radical cuts and make the changes I had sketched out. Brustein was right. These changes were desperately needed, and he was wise to avoid a direct confrontation with Walcott. That was my thankless job. We had by then developed a close working relationship, but in spite of that, it was impossible for me to steer him. Fights erupted, including one memorable one within hearing of the cast (who remained frozen onstage while Derek and I repaired to the front porch of the Hasty Pudding Theater) that included the following shouted exchange "How dare you talk to me like that? I'm 61 years old!!"—"Then act your age!!" This was a few days before we opened...

The cast of *Steel* were all experienced professionals, who knew we were underprepared. Various members of the cast approached me behind Derek's back and begged me to hold corrective rehearsals in off-hours without Derek present. I agreed to do this and we returned to the stage after Derek went home and cleaned up awkward blocking and basic common-sense movement sequences that Derek had prevented from happening. This was not good for morale. We felt shitty about it. We had the highest regard for Derek but were nonetheless exasperated by his intractability and deer-in-the-headlights helplessness. When he went home—I later figured out—he had for weeks and months been working instead on *Omeros*, which he published at almost the same time that we opened *Steel*.

In retrospect, Derek had been hoping to revive a nostalgic idea very dear to him: the *feel* of his intoxicating decade with his beloved Trinidad Theatre Workshop two decades earlier.

Trinidad was where Walcott made himself into a playwright and director. His beloved Trinidad Theatre

Steel rehearsal in Davis Square, Somerville (1991)
Galt MacDermot, Bob Scanlan, (unidentified music copyist), Derek Walcott

Bob Scanlan directing from conga drum,
with Zora (Lisa Vidal) and a child
At *Steel* rehearsal 1991

Workshop (the model for his Playwright's Theatre at Boston University) had years before gestated every one of Derek's many plays, letting each new play grow while in production—like a plant, like a child: organically, slowly, lovingly and, above all, unhurriedly. Derek's island plays were group efforts, community projects, the work of an artistic commune. Steeped in what they represented, the members of Derek's company in Trinidad played themselves.

Steel in production in Cambridge, was a transplanted Trinidad out of its element. And Derek's cast were not Trinidadians, but driven, talented, ambitious New York actors eager to succeed in a "breakthrough" musical. *Steel* as we were set up to produce it was on a fixed schedule, costing tons of rigorously managed Yankee money, for which strict accounts were to be kept. We were expected to meet daily schedules and benchmarks in our expensive rented rehearsal hall. Our production had no breathing room to find its own soul, and its soul was elsewhere in any case. No matter how much Derek tried to make our rehearsal hall *feel* like the slums of Laventille Hill, we were in reality surrounded by a crackerjack staff trained to keep us on schedule. Besieged by snow and ice (which reminded us how far we truly were from Derek's Trinidad), roaring buses, police and fire-truck sirens, and rushed, strictly timed lunch and coffee breaks... Derek persisted in "setting the tone" in rehearsal by playing his tall conga drum set up at "our" directing station. My role as director was gradually usurped by Derek's island drumming. We finally agreed to share the credit for directing, but Derek never got around to doing the basic things directors must do. Nor did he let me do them. He never "blocked" the play— and would not let me block it. The worried actors and I finally arranged, as noted above, to meet after hours, after Derek had gone home, to give some basic shape to stage movement and the flow of action on and off stage. Derek never seemed to notice the difference.

Walcott poured all his most precious personal experiences into *Steel*, which is magnificently ambitious and—(a feature of all of Walcott's work)—it is about *himself*, his own deeply embraced, deeply ambivalent colonial heritage. *Steel* remains one of Derek's best expressions of this towering theme. As he put it in one of the patois lyrics of *Steel*: "Any music, once it touch my heart, is part of my heritage."

The struggle of the divided colonial NOT to be divided was the central task Derek set for himself. In *Steel* he crafted a tale, an heroic myth, embodying the *fusion* of all his inheritances. The Trinidad *steel* pan was the perfect symbol of this theme. Hammered out of the tops of recycled and repurposed 55-gallon oil drums, they are a uniquely "native" invention made from the discards of colonial exploitation. The tuned steel pan is one of the two great musical innovations of the late twentieth century (the other is the electric guitar). As the character Growler says to Winston, "Boy you <u>born</u> for this instrument: you can't escape."

Yet Walcott's own loyalties remained torn— as *Steel* lays bare. He was in love with every thread of the tangled and irreconcilable influences that wove the history of his island home. Derek *embraced* the greater Western European-Colonial World and its high culture—in his case its British and French expressions. Like Winston Marshall in *Steel*, he also embraced that *other* culture relegated to the status of "low" and provincially "local", with its ungrammatical hybrid patois, a mixture of pidgin-English and bastard-French laced with African rhythms. These forces formed the animating spirit behind *Dream on Monkey Mountain* that had won him an Obie in 1971. They recur in his great poetic epics: *Another Life, Omeros, Tiepolo's Hound*..... *Steel* remains a vital embodiment of their author, composed with a poignant urgency in the wake of his mother's death. That massive blow hit him *while* we were working on *Steel*. Walcott found himself at a creative crossroads when he composed book and lyrics for *Steel*. And Galt was swept into one of his most effortless creative effusions: the forgotten score for *Steel* is better than the score he threw together for *Hair*.

Three Jokes

Tom Sleigh

Derek the man or Derek Walcott the poet? It's hard to know what form of address to use for someone you admire, even love, but who remains an enigma. Many people knew Derek better than I: we spoke about personal matters sometimes, but our private lives stayed private. But I don't want to get bogged down in the personal or in more or less heartfelt encomiums, the kind of sentiment that Derek once called "the standard elegiac." Banter and irreverence and more banter—those were the modes of intimacy that Derek and I seemed most at home in.

Nonetheless, our jokes and genial insults and puns signaled a kind of trust—for Derek, acting foolish and cutting up was one way to be at home with himself and other people. He assumed you could go beyond your dignity and make fun of yourself. For him, it was a form of generosity, "a mighty giving of self" in Thom Gunn's phrase. He didn't require that you meet him in the hijinks or that you match his virtuosity in telling jokes—jokes that were often revelatory of Derek's ambivalence about History as a trauma-machine that minted your poems for you and your personality to boot. But if you joined in the foolery, it helped put him at ease, because it showed that you shared some of his essential values: his complete egalitarianism, provided he felt you weren't an actual fool, in which case he'd go silent and aloof; and paradoxically, what you might call his aristocratic disdain for the overly serious, the pompous, the "professionalized" intellectual formulators. Against such people, he wrapped himself in his own isolation—an isolation that he tended to cultivate, both for the sake of his work, and because such talk sparked off a reflexive wariness in him. But when Derek felt at ease, the banter and hilarity went completely unbridled until he called it a night at 10 p.m. since he got up every morning before dawn to write.

This kind of rebellious openness and irreverence is perhaps best illustrated in a joke I heard Derek tell many times, always with the same delight in the reversal of roles, the skewering of pieties both religious and social. The Pope is blessing the multitudes in St. Peter's Square when a little boy runs out of the crowd and, standing all alone before the vast flock of the Faithful, stares and stares and stares at the Pope until he finally shouts out, "Fuck you, Pope!" To which the Pope replies, "Little boy, do you know who I am? I am the Bishop of Rome, the Vicar of Christ, Successor of the Prince of the Apostles, Supreme Pontiff of the Universal Church. So no, little boy—fuck you!" Whether you find this funny or not, it reveals something essential about both the man and the poet. The verbal exuberance of both Pope and little boy in telling each other off is linked to what Walcott called the "Adamic view" of humanity in his essay "The Muse of History."

By Adamic, Walcott means a New World poetic impulse which rejects "servitude to the muse of history," and which refuses to produce "a literature of recrimination and despair, a literature of revenge written by the descendants of slaves or a literature of remorse written by the descendants of masters." Instead, he envisions a literature of primal "exuberance," in which the poet is still "capable of enormous wonder."

To ground all this in Derek's joke, one could say that both Pope and little boy are, in the act of utterance, suddenly released from the mind-forged manacles that makes one a Pope and the other a comparatively helpless little boy. Each one's "fuck you" signals a different kind of freedom, even a transgression: in the little boy's case, his trespass is not only one of bad manners and, depending on his parents, bad morals, but it's also a linguistic declaration of war against all things made hoary and tediously respectable through custom and convention. His *Fuck you!* is a verbally insouciant revolt against the coercive nature of social expectation, whether in habits of devotion or linguistic pieties. And in the Pope's case, after his flight of high rhetoric in enumerating his titles, his *Fuck you!* undercuts his own authority even as it contrasts two different registers of speech, the officialese of sanctioned culture in collision with the down-home language of the street. For all that the Pope seems like a figure of almost omnipotent power in relation to the little boy, underneath the joke is how both

Pope and little boy meet in their linguistic delight in casting off, if only momentarily, their expected habits of language and behavior.

On a political level, you can construe both Pope and little boy as Walcott's version of colonial history, in which the linguistic revolt of both is a revolt against what Walcott calls the muse of history. The two *fuck yous* overleap history by insisting on the human capacity to step out of papal robes, chasubles, albs, and miters—all the trappings of worldly power—as well as to step beyond the obedient demeanor of "good" little boys. And for a moment, as one laughs, the language feels refreshed. And even if you don't laugh, and find the joke a little jejune, which it assuredly is, nonetheless those two fuck yous, and the timing with which they are delivered, imitate the structure of a poem in its verbal surprises and reversals, even if they fall short of our usual assumptions about poetry's linguistic range and capabilities. Freed from the deadening weight of costume and proscribed behavior, poetic utterance manifests "the miracle of possibility which every poet demonstrates."

Which is not to say that the Pope isn't culpable as a potential oppressor. But for Walcott, it isn't so much the social position as the poetic disposition that he's interested in understanding. By the same token, no one could have a finer appreciation for the burden of a colonial past than Walcott when he writes:

The vision, the "democratic vistas," is not metaphorical, it is a social necessity. A political philosophy rooted in elation would have to accept belief in a second Adam, the re-creation of the entire order, from religion to the simplest domestic rituals. The myth of the noble savage would not be revived, for that myth never emanated from the savage but has always been the nostalgia of the Old

World, its longing for innocence. The great poetry of the New World does not pretend to such innocence, its vision is not naïve. Rather, like its fruits, its savour is a mixture of the acid and the sweet, the apples of its second Eden have the tartness of experience. In such poetry there is a bitter memory and it is the bitterness that dries last on the tongue. It is the acidulous that supplies its energy. The golden apples of this sun are shot with acid.... For us in the archipelago, the tribal memory is salted with the bitter memory of migration.

Bitter acid on Walcott's tongue as his colonial inheritance is something to both spit out and to savor. This is beautifully exemplified by his affection for both Aimé Césaire and Saint-John Perse who in tandem illustrate in a more literarily formal way the dynamic between the muse of history and poetic utterance. Walcott writes:

If we think of one as poor and the other as privileged when we read their addresses to the New World, if we must see one as black and one as white, we are not only dividing this sensibility by the process of the sociologist, we are denying the range of either poet, the power of compassion and the power of fury.

Walcott would be sympathetic to the view expressed by his friend Seamus Heaney that if poetry is to survive as its own independent form of consciousness, it cannot be subservient to literary criticism, politics, religion, or sociology, even as it partakes of all of them. In his essay "The Redress of Poetry," Heaney writes, "Poetry,...whether it belongs to an old political dispensation or aspires to express a new one, has to be a working model of inclusive consciousness.... As long as the coordinates of the imagined thing correspond to those of the world that we live in and endure, poetry is fulfilling its counter weighting function." And for Walcott, both Saint-John Perse and Aimé Césaire are part of that New World model of inclusive consciousness. And lest anyone accuse Walcott of a kind of dopey "we're all in this together" humanism, he states unequivocally of his passion for both Perse and Césaire that he

> is not making out a case for assimilation and for the common simplicity of all men; we are interested in their differences, openly, but what astonishes us in both poets is their elation, their staggering elation in possibility. And one is not talking of a possible ideal society, for you will find that only in the later work of Perse, a society which is inaccessible by its very grandeur, but of the elation in presences which exists in Éloges and Pour fêter une enfance... As the language of Perse later becomes hammered and artificial, so does the rhetoric of Césaire move towards the heraldic, but their first great work is as deeply rooted and supple as a vine.

For all Walcott's admiration of both poets, he is clear-eyed about their limitations and how each one moves from being a figure of Adamic utterance, the lovechild of linguistic discovery, to their own incarnations of papal authority vested in settled notions about language and social hierarchy.

But if we see in Césaire and Perse two enabling elders before they ossified into self-parody, no poem of Walcott's better illustrates both poets' linguistic inclusiveness than his vernacular masterpiece, "The Schooner Flight." The fact that his forebears' poems are written in French doesn't invalidate what Walcott learned from them in tuning his ear to both the dissonant strains of demotic frequencies, as well as the big booming English line as it comes down to him through Spenser, Sidney, and Shakespeare. Like that inheritance, Walcott's English in "The Schooner Flight" is a wonderfully flexible amalgam of ordinary St. Lucian speech and literary allusiveness; as Walcott says of his mixed race / archipelago / colonially educated / street smart heritage, "… either I'm nobody, or I'm a nation." And because the poem oscillates between the language of the street and Césaire and Perse, the Jacobean and Elizabethan playwrights, Dante and Homer (the tercet used in *Omeros* is an obvious homage to Dante, while the title itself insists on continuities between the Caribbean archipelago and the Greek one), "The Schooner Flight" thrives on adapting iambic pentameter and terminal rhyme to suit the polymathic, polynational, polyvocal mouth of Shabine, Walcott's able-bodied and able-tongued seaman alter-ego. Here is what you might call the poem's overture, written in an idiom that is totally distinctive Walcott, an idiom drawn from the "bare ruined choirs" of the Jacobean playwrights and Elizabethan song, but with complete filial devotion to the St. Lucian *demos*:

In idle August, while the sea soft
and leaves of brown islands stick to the rim
of this Caribbean, I blow out the light
by the dreamless face of Maria Concepcion
to ship as a seaman on the schooner Flight.
Out in the yard turning gray in the dawn,
I stood like a stone and nothing else move
but the cold sea rippling like galvanize
and the nail holes of stars in the sky roof,
till a wind start to interfere with the trees.
I pass me dry neighbor sweeping she yard

as I went downhill, and I nearly said:
"sweep soft, you witch, 'cause she don't sleep hard,"
but the bitch look through me like I was dead.
A route taxi pull up, park-lights still on.
The driver size up my bags with a grin:
"This time, Shabine, like you really gone!"
I ain't answer the ass, I simply pile in
the back seat and watch the sky burn
above Laventille pink as the gown
in which the woman I left was sleeping,
and I look in the rearview and see a man
exactly like me, and the man was weeping
for the houses, the streets, that whole fucking island.

....

You ever look up from some lonely beach
and see a far schooner? Well, when I write
this poem, each phrase go be soaked in salt;
I go draw and knot every line as tight
as ropes in this rigging; in simple speech
my common language go be the wind,
my pages the sails of the schooner Flight.
But let me tell you how this business begin.

In this extended passage Walcott's ear traversing effortlessly from the slant rhyme between "move" and "galvanize" signals his total at-homeness in both demotic usage and the language derived from what he calls, in a deeply ambivalent essay on V. S. Naipaul, the islands' "small but excellent libraries (since they could afford only the classics)." Unlike Naipaul, whose career was marked by a turning away from his West Indian heritage to a full-fledged embrace of his Britishness and his eventual knighthood, Walcott (also knighted) was neither worried or wrong-footed by either San Lucian speech or the language of the classics:

> ...once I had decided to make the writing of poetry my life, my actual, not my imaginative life, I felt both a rejection and a fear of Europe while I learned its poetry. I have remained this way, but the emotions have changed, they are subtler, more controlled, for I would no longer wish to visit Europe as if I could repossess it than I would wish to visit Africa for that purpose... I felt, I knew, that if I went to England I would never become a poet, far more a West Indian, and that was the only thing I could see myself becoming, a West Indian poet. The language I used did not bother me. I had given it, and it was irretrievably given; I could no more give it back than they could claim it.

You can see this givenness in operation in the imagistically wrought, but beautifully casual spokenness of the foregoing passage, especially in its concluding lines:

> I go draw and knot every line as tight
> as ropes in this rigging; in simple speech
> my common language go be the wind,
> my pages the sails of the schooner Flight.

As the wind begins to swell the sails, and the schooner Flight heaves to and heads out to sea, the metaphor is subsumed by what Walcott calls "simple speech"; but his use of a demotic phrase like "go be the wind" helps to naturalize the idiom so that when the pages turn into sails, every shift in vocal tone is perfectly matched by an imagistic one, a perfection of intention and execution which is difficult to achieve, even as it insists on its own verbal transparency. This is writing of a high order which doesn't insist on itself. Instead, its equilibrium is calibrated to the early example of Perse and Césaire, in which every verbal gesture has a naturalness and rootedness that springs out of two perfectly understood impulses—the impulse to enter into one's own culture as a grateful, but proud inheritor, as well as becoming "omnivorous about the art and literature of Europe to understand my own world." Thus the Pope and the little boy can relax into mutual laughter, not so much at each other's expense, but at the wonder of how language can bridge what would otherwise be (and in most worldly contexts is) an unbridgeable gap. It's not that the gap doesn't open up again the instant that one finishes reading the poem, but "the steadfastness of speech articulation," as Osip Mandelstam once called it, gives a momentary access to a freshened perspective that might, just might, become the world-shifting fulcrum that can move us beyond our limitations to a more comprehensive fellow feeling.

Which brings me to my second joke.

A very posh Englishman has been castaway for years and years on a desert island when suddenly out to sea he spots a sail that gets larger and larger until it anchors just off shore, and the captain and a few members of his crew lower the long boat and row to where the Englishman is yelling and waving to them. "Hello chaps!" he shouts, "jolly good of you to come to my island! I've been waiting years and years for you and finally you're here. But before you take me onboard, let me show you my island and my little manor house. It's bloody *mahvelous*, isn't it?" But what the sailors see is a tumble down shack made of split bamboo and battered palm fronds; yet they nod appreciatively and struggle to find the right words, so that the old gent, carried away by his own enthusiasm, says, "And now, lads, let me

show you the rest of my island, and especially my club—
it's a splendid place, I must say, very exclusive, only the
crème de la crème allowed. Now come along!" So they
stumble through the bush in the brutal heat for a couple of
miles while the old man gesticulates enthusiastically at the
scenery and the so-called "views," but as they walk along,
the seamen notice another ruined little shack off by itself
on a promontory—a shack which is in every way identical
to the manor, so that only the old man, who in any case is
the island's sole inhabitant, could have built it. But since
the old gent says nothing about it, they keep hacking their
way through the vines until they reach the top of a little hill
and there, nestled in scrub jungle, is what the old man calls
his club: but it, too, is an even more dilapidated version
of the "manor." By this time the captain has had enough,
so he suggests that they proceed directly to the ship. But
on the way back, curiosity grips him, as well as a desire
to flatter the old man's delusions, and so he says as they
pass the promontory, "I say, sir, what is that magnificent
building over there? You haven't told us about it yet." But
the old man says nothing and so the captain repeats his
question, and thinking that the old fellow may be hard
of hearing or has become suddenly a little shy, says quite
loudly, "Sir, please do tell us about it!" But the old man
shakes his head, grumbles and growls, and refuses to say
anything so that the seamen, encouraged by a wink from
the captain, start asking him too. And finally the old man,
with a frown and shrug of complete social superiority,
snorts, "Hmmph…that awful place? Well, all I can tell you
is that it's NOT my club."

I know, I know…a lot of verbiage for what seems like
a dig at English snobbery. But whenever Derek told this
joke, I was struck by two things: by his relish for playing an
upper class twit, no doubt a twit who could have made his

money through a sugar plantation worked by slaves who
might well be Derek's ancestors; and by Derek's feeling for
the old gent's idiom, just how tonally accurate and nuanced
it was even as parody. This feeling for the theatricality of
language, as well as Derek's keen sense of history as a force
you outstripped by poetic speech, rather than a force you
succumbed to (or even worse, subjected yourself to), were
dual impulses that grew ever stronger in Derek's work.

In *The Fortunate Traveller*, the book he published after
The Star-Apple Kingdom, Walcott's interest in persona united
these two impulses. His old gent in the joke morphed in
The Star-Apple Kingdom into an infinitely more elaborated
version of his colonial persona, Koenig, in "Koenig of the
River." And then Koenig, a belated, ineffectual missionary
of empire, who Walcott shruggingly acknowledges is
nothing but a poetic fiction, further morphs in *The Fortunate
Traveller* into an uprooted cosmopolite citizen of the world.
This citizen is what the old man's island consciousness
could never have imagined—an intelligence from outside
his narrow concerns about what is and isn't his club. In
fact, Walcott would be the old gent's nightmare—not only a
Caliban without a trace of inferiority, but a Caliban obsessed
with the decolonialization of the West Indies and Africa.
As the waning hangover of what Walcott's quasi-diplomat
speaker of "The Fortunate Traveller" calls "the imperial
fiction" keeps on throbbing with its interminable headache,
the poet struggles to find a vantage from which to stay true
to his antipathy to the myth of historically determined
personalities and fates, even as his poems become more
and more obsessed with balancing matters of state against
matters of the heart...especially in the marital sphere.

However, in *The Fortunate Traveller* there's an implicit
disconnect between the world of the domestic and the
way Walcott's eye can't help but focus on the political

horizon going up in flames. For all Walcott's verbal muscle and grace, the shifts in scale between the home front and the front-line depredations of historical struggle feel provocatively out of kilter with their own means. The poems navigate this unease such that the language, for all its brilliance, occasionally seems on the verge of hardening into rhetoric—but never quite. Nonetheless, the recurrent references to the Holocaust, the dastard operation of international capital as embodied by the World Bank, the Cold War spy vs. spy of arms-dealers posing as tractor salesmen, etc., seems always on the verge of turning into a kind of post-modern, headline-driven pageantry.

But then something miraculous begins to happen: the poet's marital disintegrations, his concern for his children, and his own self-reckonings begin to weave their way into the lightly fictionalized personas until finally all there is is the poet's own face, the only mask the mask of language. Walcott's freedom from the old gent's historical exactions, as well as a flowering of self-sufficiency, seems to free the poet to dispense with personas entirely, and to write as close to his nerves as he would ever write in the casual sounding, but beautifully wrought poems in his next book, *Midsummer*—a book in which no poem goes longer than a page, and in which the lines have a loose pentameter ease that heralds a fresh linguistic impulse *Nel mezzo del cammin de nostra vita*. Of these poems, Walcott said he wanted them to have the look of a jacket draped casually over a chair— and in their meandering associations and cumulative sweep, they move with loose-limbed assurance through all their difficult self-reckonings both private and public.

In this book, alter-egos and personae are foregone, or are so totally assimilated to Walcott's own voice that they're rendered unnecessary. His anxiety about history has suddenly come into alignment with his faith in poetic utterance as a way to overbear it. All is late summer light, brilliant illuminations of ordinary domestic scenes. The breaking of waves and the sweep of lines down the page become mirror images of each other. From line to line, the flux of daily life sorts with the atrocities of history. The meditative looseness of these poems gathers up details of San Lucian life, from its coconut fronds to its Chinese laundries to the elemental facts of stone, sea, wind, and branch.

At the same time, *Midsummer* bristles with an allusiveness that comprehends Walcott's nostalgia for a world culture which he can draw on as his own self-made, self-willed inheritance. Of his schoolboy infatuation with English poetry, he once said in an interview in *The Guardian* that his reaction to wanting to be a poet "was the very same as an English schoolboy...: to take models that were in literature—Auden, MacNeice, Dylan Thomas—and make them your own. They were immediately accessible, with no feeling of alienation about it..." Well, good work if you can get it. That wasn't what every writer of Walcott's generation felt—it's a literary truism that a writer like Kamau Brathwaite, and his ambition to fashion what he called "nation language" is Walcott's polar opposite. But Brathwaite, like Walcott, also read T. S. Eliot and turned him to his own peculiar uses. So maybe they aren't as far apart as their public pronouncements might seem to make them.

That said, Walcott's affection for individual English poets doesn't mean that he wasn't deeply suspicious of any other standard of poetic achievement than Mandelstam's assertion of poetry as "the steadfastness of speech articulation." In referring to the Brixton riots of the 1980s (or uprisings, depending on your point of view), he writes:

Praise had bled my lines white of any more anger,
and snow had inducted me into white fellowships,

while Calibans howled down the barred streets of an empire that began with Caedmon's raceless dew, and is ending in the alleys of Brixton, burning like Turner's ships.

You can indict these lines for their literary aloofness in describing Brixtonites as "Calibans," as opposed to ordinary people fed up with police harassment, poor housing, and unemployment, not to mention Maggie Thatcher's stop and search laws, and her statement that the UK might eventually be "swamped by people of a different culture." But the last two lines are more ambiguous, harder to pin down. For if Caedmon, the so-called first English poet, a cowherd, is aligned with the freshness of dew, and the elemental forces of wind, rain, and sun that inhere to no species, let alone race, then Walcott's assertion that Caedmon's legacy has ended in the flames of empire "burning like Turner's ships" amounts to a fierce indictment of imperial Britannia's betrayal of Caedmon's originary, poetic vitality. It seems to me that both Caedmon's potential, and the betrayal of it, hover above this passage and perfectly enact Walcott's ambivalence about his own roots and his relative success. Artistically, he might be said to have a right to keep faith with his schoolboy crushes; while politically, you can hit him hard as being too distant from ordinary realities...but is he enthralled to either possibility? Or is he enacting a profound ambivalence that refuses resolution?

That ambiguous seesawing back and forth, always searching for equilibrium but never quite achieving it, is one of the qualities that suffuses *Midsummer* from beginning to end. Poem after poem stages his confrontation with his own heritage, the history of empire, and the primal delight he experiences in wind, sea, and sky. The exacerbation of his conscience for having allowed praise to bleed his "lines white of any more anger", even as he's being inducted into "white fellowships/while Calibans howled down the barred streets of an empire" gives no one an easy out, least of all himself. The questions keep nagging: are these ordinary people really Calibans? Is the speaker of this poem a sell-out, culpable for his seeming remove? Am I as a white-skinned reader and commentator too close to my version of Derek and too far from Brixton realities in the 1980s to be reliable?

But these difficult questions are for me what makes *Midsummer* such a galvanizing book. In these lines from "IX" Walcott writes:

> …The lines that jerk
> into step do not fit any mold. More than time
> keeps shifting. Language never fits geography
> except when the earth and summer lightning rhyme.
> When I was greener, I strained with a branch
> to utter every tongue, language, and life at once.
> More skillful now, I'm more dissatisfied.
> They never align, nature and your
> own nature. Too rapid the lightning's shorthand,
> too patient the sea repeatedly tearing up paper,
> too frantic the wind unravelling the same knot,
> too slow the stones crawling toward language every night.

Here Walcott directly confronts the mismatch between whatever language you fashion into your own and the world that is always slipping out of gear, which leaves your formulations perennially misaligned, no matter your intentions or your skill. And then when you get older, you suddenly see how wrong-headed it was to think that the purpose of poetry was to find some kind of alignment between self and world. As Walcott says, "They never align, nature and your/own nature." But even as he baldly admits the insufficiency of his, or anyone's, poetic achievement, he effects in the passage's last four lines a truly stunning reciprocity between language and sea, wind, and stone. Nothing in *Midsummer* hardens into the reliable, upper case Certainties that in Randall Jarrell's phrase "go perpetually by perpetually on time," and that mar the late work of Perse and Césaire. Instead, the sea tears up the paper your poem is written on, the wind unravels every knot—and yet the stones crawling up the beach toward you at night call out for definition and impress upon you, in a wholly secular way, the inspired and inspiriting Caedmon-like sense of poetic vocation.

Which brings me to the third and final joke.

Jesus and the disciples are seated at the Last Supper, when Jesus says to them, "By dawn tomorrow one of you will betray me." The disciples are horrified and Peter jumps up from the table and bends down before Jesus and says, "Is it me, Lord, is it me?" And Jesus says in a grave, deep voice, "No, Peter, it is not you." And then John kneels down before him and says in a voice choked with tears, "Is it me, Lord, is it me?" And Jesus says, "No, John, it is not you." And eventually one by one the disciples kneel in front of him, each one asking him in an agonized voice, tears pouring down their faces, "Is it me, Lord, is it me?" And to disciple after disciple Jesus says in the same grave, deep voice, "No, it is not you." And finally Judas kneels down, and outdoing all the others in his weeping and sorrow, says, "Is it me, Lord, is it me?" And Jesus scrunches up his face in mockery of Judas's tears, and says in an irritating, high whiny voice, "Is it *ME*, Lord, is it *ME*?"

OK…this is probably the least obviously funny joke of all three, so I'll simply say you had to be there. Rather than this joke being emblematic of a particular book or moment in Walcott's career, I want to suggest that the formality, not to say pomposity, of Jesus and his disciples in their mutual interrogations, was a life-long stylistic temptation for Derek. And yet there was always the gyroscopic rightness of his feel for spoken idiom bringing him back to the vertical, the upright, but not uptight, way of saying it. His language, for all its spit and polish and calibrated shine, nonetheless keeps faith with his antic Jesus mocking not only Judas's, but his own self-seriousness. You might say that Jesus in mocking himself is the backlash of Derek's own tongue against Derek Walcott the Nobel Laureate, the Éminence Grise. He never lost sight of his own fallible humanity, and in one of his best later books (and my personal favorite), *The Bounty*, published in 1997, thirteen years after *Midsummer*, he plumbs that fallen sense of himself in a series of poems that cut so close to the bone that they are unparalleled in his career for their directness and integrity of feeling.

By this time in his career, stentorian Jesus and histrionic Judas have both been chastened, but not silenced by salutary self-mockery. Like *Midsummer*, *The Bounty* mainly consists of short meditations, none longer than a page. Again the prosody is a long, loose pentameter line, casually rhymed or not, in which the elaborated syntax follows what Elizabeth Bishop once called "the mind in motion." All this is admirably on display in "5/Parang", which seems paradigmatic of the book's virtues as a whole. The poem is in three parts, each elaborating a pain in the mind that stems from betrayal: the betrayal of memory in *i*, the betrayal inherent in domestic love in *ii*, and self-betrayal in *iii*. As to the precise nature of these betrayals, despite Robert Lowell's injunction, "Yet why not say what happened?", Walcott has never been straightforward in directly autobiographical ways (neither, for that matter, was Lowell: as he once said in an interview, the art of autobiography is to give readers the impression that they are "getting the real 'Robert Lowell'"). As close as Derek comes to giving us the real "Derek Walcott" is to confess in *ii* that he is "under intense mental pain", and to acknowledge in *iii* in the final lines that his has been "a life of incredible errors." The typical response here would be to say, *Join the club!* But even if we knew the circumstances, what would they add to what amounts to a cri de coeur sans autobiographical detail? Rather than distract us with Judas or Jesus in their stagey ritual of guilt and condemnation, Walcott shifts the focus to what you might call the underlying psychological structure of what he feels:

> Days change, the sunlight goes, then it returns, and wearily,
> under intense mental pain, I remember a corner
> of brilliant Saddle Road coming out of the valley
> of leaf-quiet Santa Cruz, a passage with a bridge, one the
> desperate memory fastens on even as it passes all the
> other possible places; why this particular one?
>
> ......
> ...Because memory is less
> than the place which it cherishes, frames itself from nowhere
> except to say that even with the shit and the stress
> of what we do to each other, the running stream's bliss
> contradicts the self-importance of despair
> by these glittering simplicities, water, leaves, and air,
> that elate dissolution which goes beyond happiness.

I hear in this the voice of Judas in the aftermath of his betrayal, pondering and analyzing, trying to understand what could have possessed him to make such a terrible error. What is psychologically revelatory in this passage is how the rhymes among "less" "stress" "bliss" and "happiness" seem to propose an alternative universe to the rhyme between "nowhere" and "despair"; but then the next rhyme of that triad, "air," brings both sets of rhymes into a tentative resolution between self-reflexive regret and the Judas-like self-importance of despair, and those "glittering simplicities, water, leaves, and air" of the natural world.

But what is most impressive about these lines is the spoken ease Walcott has achieved in writing about personally painful subjects, while still maintaining a sense of reticence and emotional decorum. Before *The Bounty*, he rarely allowed himself such a bald, homely statement as "even with the shit and the stress/of what we do to each other." This is Jesus's mockery of Judas's rhetoric but shorn of any satiric intent. Instead, it's the plain-spoken testimony of a mind under such terrible pressure that it's almost inarticulate. It reminds me of Bishop's "Crusoe in England," in which the poem's climactic moment isn't the bravura descriptive writing of "islands spawning islands,/like frogs' eggs turning into polliwogs/of islands," or of waterspouts likened to "Glass chimneys, flexible, attenuated,/sacerdotal beings of glass," but the heartbroken avowal in the poem's plain-spoken final lines: "—And Friday, my dear Friday, died of measles/ seventeen years ago come March." Unlike Bishop, Walcott has no need of a Crusoe through which to channel his mental suffering. After all, he's an island dweller, not a castaway; and if he's to find any resolution or relief or perspective on "the shit and the stress," then he will have to find it in San Lucia, his home ground. There are no island paradises or hells for his thoughts to escape to.

That said, the poet isn't so much looking for resolution as self-understanding; and in that need Walcott, without quite intending to, has been led by his scrutiny of his own suffering to what Czeslaw Milosz once called "the general human perspective"—that is, the way any one person, in Adrienne Rich's words, finds a legitimate means "to connect, without hysteria," one's individual pain to the collective pain of the world. In contrast to the worldly shit and stress of all human action, the poet experiences in the following lines a sudden enlargement of consciousness, in which the repetition of "it" in the first line refers to the slippery operations of memory as it dissolves into death:

> Perhaps because it disembodies, it neutralises distance
> and the shadows of leaves on the road and the bridge
>   in the sun,
> proving that it will remain in any of two directions,
> leaving life and approaching the calm of extinction
> with the blissful indifference with which a small stream
> runs alongside the bridge and the flecked hills of Paramin....

In this passage the waters of death and the waters of life flow together. To drink from that stream is to drink deep the "blissful indifference" not of human mortality but of elemental cycles of rain, sun, and the shadows of leaves playing over the road and the bridge that crosses those waters. For where all this stress and shit must end is in that "blissful indifference." The rhetoric of Judas and the anti-rhetoric of Jesus are both left behind in the fading of memory.

Finally, what the poet is left with is his need to celebrate the humanity of his fellow islanders:

> In short, this affection for what is simple and known,
> the direct faces, the deprived but resigned ones
> whom you have exalted: are they utterly your own
> as surely as your shadow is a thing of the sun's?

In Walcott's devotion to the "direct faces" of "the deprived but resigned ones," he leaves behind the dragging memory of his own "intense mental pain." But when he questions if his desire to exalt them has, in fact, made them "utterly your own," he seems to suspect himself of a kind of poetic hubris: just because he feels "affection for what is simple and known" is no guarantee that that affection will be acknowledged, let alone returned, or that being "simple and known" is as transparent as it seems. And so he lets the question hang, unresolved, and in that irresolution, the poet suddenly finds himself reduced to his own shadow, as much "a thing of the sun's" as the "small stream" and "the flecked hills of Paramin." And as his anguish recedes into "the calm of extinction," what comes forward is the presence of the world itself: "the night grows its velvet, the frogs croak/behind fences, the dogs bark at ghosts." For all his hopeful, humane embrace of his fellow islanders, it's only among the ghosts and in "that elate dissolution which goes beyond happiness" that he finds the ultimate sign of our shared humanity.

MEMORIES OF DEREK WALCOTT

Kate Snodgrass

I used to fly every year to St. Lucia in January to take part in celebrating Derek's birthday (Jan. 23). I brought him a sable brush for his watercolors. Traditionally, the island celebrates his birthday with an entire week of poetry and play readings, a celebration at the Governor-General's House, and ending finally with the "Nobel Speech"—given by literary luminaries such as Rosanna Warren, Caryl "Caz" Phillips, Glyn Maxwell, Jamaica Kincaid. Many of Derek's friends would travel from all over the world to celebrate with him as well, and I was among those hangers-on. We were a staunch, if mismatched, band of writers from all over the world—Boston, Spain, China, Italy, England, India, Transylvania, Canada. Derek and his partner Sigrid would take us to dinner and honor us with a boat ride down to Soufrière on the west coast of the island. On the boat, we swayed to reggae music and sipped the undrinkable pink punch (the only liquid offered on the boat) until we stopped for lunch at the Ladera Resort above the Pitons. Then we traversed back up the coast to Castries, stopping for a late-afternoon dip in the Caribbean Sea. By sunset, we were sunburned and sated. It was a kind of heaven.

But the last celebration before his death in March, 2017, Derek was physically frail, and he could not make the boat trip down the island, so all of us wandered Rodney Bay, cast adrift and more lost than found. We sampled the tourist bars, traced the beaches, and sat on Derek's veranda waiting for him to rise from his nap. Caz Phillips and Glyn Maxwell, perhaps his dearest friends then, and I sat with him… "What one thing do you love about this island?" he demanded of me. I replied, "You." "No, no, aside from me!" (I knew there was no right answer to this.) I stuttered out, "I love the sound of the sea." We could hear it from where we were sitting. He was silent, and then…"That is so cliché." We cannot separate Derek from St. Lucia— this stunningly beautiful and deeply flawed rain forest of an island suffering from all the classic Caribbean riches, such as crime, poverty, corruption—an island existing on tourism, volcanic rock, colonized by the Spanish, French, and British and with a language blending an Englishman's drawl with a French patois. Derek was and will always be St. Lucia to me.

I am not alone in loving Derek, but those of us who loved him did so at our own risk. As complicated as his island, Derek was brilliant and charismatic, an inordinately generous friend, and a prodigious lover of puns. To wit: "A mushroom walks into a bar. 'Anybody want a date? I'm a real fun guy.'" Besides this questionable sense of humor (don't get me wrong—I counted it a good day when I could make Derek laugh), he was also knotty and mercurial. Rooted in what I believe was a true shyness, he was oddly inept in social situations, and he could be boyish and petulant when he didn't get his way. Derek played the bongos. He loved cats. He proudly professed himself a "crier" and was easily moved to tears when something touched him, which was often in his later years. Months after the unexpected death of his great friend Seamus Heaney, he would break down at a mention, a memory. It was an endearing quality given his standing in the world of the literati. No sucking it up for Derek. He let everything out. He wore his heart on his sleeve like a talisman.

Many of us who came to celebrate Derek's birthday were his students at one time or another. We were representative of hundreds—maybe thousands—of writers whom Derek mentored over the years, and we hung onto his mentorship like a guarded jewel: "Yes, I worked with Derek Walcott." I was lucky enough to audit his playwriting classes for 20 years at Boston University where he taught playwriting and poetry in the Creative Writing Department. As a teacher, Derek was demanding, curious, and uncompromising. The inevitable story students continue to pass down is about one unlucky playwright who sat through an entire semester hearing only the first line of his play (and he was not alone in this). It was no joke. Derek viewed a play as something to be fleshed out and shaped, and he knew that the playwrights must know everything about the worlds they create. If the beginning of the play doesn't work, chances are the rest of the play won't either. That's a hard lesson for those of us who love the sound of our own voice, but I have held onto this in my own writing and teaching. Derek was always, always right.

Derek's Boston Playwrights' Theatre was born from his desire to teach playwriting at Boston University because, I suspect, he missed the "family" of the Trinidad Theatre Workshop mightily. Thankfully, we were honored to produce a number of Derek's plays over the years—the mysterious and powerful *Dream on Monkey Mountain* and the joyous *The Joker of Seville* in collaboration with his Trinidad Theatre Workshop. We produced *Pantomime*, and the cautionary folk-tale *Ti-Jean and His Brothers*. We premiered *Walker, a Play with Music*, Derek's theatrical investigation of the life and death of abolitionist David Walker. And we workshopped his plays over the years— *The Odyssey, Ghost Dance, Viva Detroit!* He used Theatre as a workshop, and to him it was a shelter. It has been a gift to me and to my life in the Theatre to learn from Derek, to see his constant revisions, his forced compromises, his failures, and his successes. His plays are just like the man himself—huge, full of complexities and humor, musical, and deeply human.

One of my last memories of Derek is him sitting on his veranda with a young poet, Pigeon Island some small distance across the sea, talking through the young man's initial drafts. Derek gave back into the caldron from which we all were stirred. He demanded focus and forgave youth. He understood that we will all get better if, and only if, we keep writing. His passion never wavered, and he taught by example. I am grateful for it all. I remember the call for excellence, the demand for truth. And I miss the bad jokes; I miss his laughter. I miss his mind in the world with us. "When he left the beach the sea was still going on" (*Omeros* by Derek Walcott).

"UNKNOWN TO THE POLICE":

WALCOTT AS TEACHER

Jacob Strautmann

Once, Derek asked the poets—I was among them in 1999 at Boston University—to visit him later that morning at his Boston Playwrights' Theatre because, as he told us, "The American Theater needs poets." He also said, going a little too far, "You are already good poets, so you must be good playwrights." We showed up to see what he intended to do with us, completely unconvinced, and discovered he had also invited professional actors from the Boston theater community. He asked them to run part of the final scene of *A Streetcar Named Desire*.

Blanche is battered and now lost to her terror of being taken away. Stella is weeping. "What have I done to my sister." Mitch throws a punch at Stanley. The Matron from the institution has just fought off Blanche's attack and is holding her arms behind her. She says, "These fingernails have to be trimmed." She suggests they get the straight jacket. The doctor takes off his hat, says "only if it's necessary." He calls her Ms. Dubois. He is suddenly kind, and Blanche sees it. She asks to be let go. The doctor allows it, and, with her hands free, Ms. Blanche Dubois reaches for him and says, "Whoever you are -- I've always depended on the kindness of strangers." Derek stopped the actors, said to them more than us, "Did you hear? That's loose iambic pentameter." He counted it out. "I've al/ ways depend/ ed on/ the kind/ ness of strang/ ers." We nodded. The actors waited.

He then asked Blanche to run the scene again, except this time, instead of the lines we all knew by heart, she was to use lines from an American poet of equal caliber. Derek chose the Ohio-born James Wright and his "The Minneapolis Poem" about suicides and drunks in the Mississippi River. It didn't matter that the subject dovetailed or didn't. It was American. It was beautiful. It was the poetry of Williams's theatrical moment that mattered, and it *was* poetry.

And so, Stella weeps, Stanley fights Mitch, Blanche attacks, the Matron says, "These fingernails have to be trimmed." The Doctor is kind. With her hands free, she reaches for him; Ms. Blanche Dubois recites Wright's "I want to be lifted up / by some great white bird unknown to the police." Derek turned around to look at us poets blinking from the darkness, and then back to the Boston actors he was so fond of, as if to say, "See what I mean?"

DEREK WALCOTT:

POETRY AND THE POWERS

Rosanna Warren

In his Nobel lecture, Derek Walcott took up once again the age-old question of the impotence and the power of poetry: "Survival is the triumph of stubbornness, and spiritual stubbornness, a sublime stupidity, is what makes the occupation of poetry endure, when there are so many things that should make it futile." Poetry may seem futile when pitted against armies, government, taxes, political corruption, wealth, ideology, religion, social media...You make your own list of the powers you think rule the world. Ever since Plato cast poets out of the Republic, lovers of poetry have been trying to defend it. And Plato really paid poetry a compliment by treating it as so dangerous it needed to be cast out. More damaging to poetry is Walcott's suggestion that it's pointless. Futile. Not even worth casting out.

Yeats and Auden both struggled with the question of poetry's power and lack of power. Both were thrown, willy nilly, into eras when brute power was being exercised all around them, when History reared up in a seizure—Yeats in the struggles of Irish independence, Auden in the convulsions of Socialism, Fascism, Stalinism, and World War II. Each recognized in himself an almost shamanic gift to rouse audiences through language; recognized, that is, a power in poetry. Auden, more than Yeats, came to distrust that power. Walcott has inherited from both Yeats and Auden, and he too has worried in book after book about poetry's relation to power.

As a moony, *fin-de-siècle* bard—perhaps because he *was* a moony, *fin-de-siècle* bard—Yeats in 1899 pondered the world's contempt for the work of poetry in the poem "Adam's Curse."

> I said: 'A line will take us hours maybe;
> Yet if it does not seem a moment's thought,
> Our stitching and unstitching has been naught.
> Better go down upon your marrow bones
> And scrub a kitchen pavement, or break stones
> Like an old pauper, in all kinds of weather;
> For to articulate sweet sounds together
> Is to work harder than all these, and yet
> Be thought an idler by the noisy set
> Of bankers, schoolmasters, and clergymen
> The martyrs call the world...'

Embracing his anti-self and toughening himself by writing plays, Yeats devised a language of such force he sent the bankers, schoolmasters, and clergymen rolling head over heels into the "dolphin-torn, the gong-tormented sea." Auden, coming later, mistrusted Yeats's word magic, all the more so as he himself practiced word magic and found he was good at it, notoriously in the propagandistic poem "Spain" with its "conscious acceptance of guilt in the necessary murder"— a poem he grew ashamed of and banished from his *Collected Poems*. In another banished poem, "September 1, 1939," Auden, having recently arrived in New York, contemplated the outbreak of massive war, and flirted still with the notion that the poet, even in his frailty and singularity, might exert some counter-power to the world's monstrosity: "All I have is a voice / To undo the folded lie." But already in that fateful year, 1939, in his elegy for Yeats, uneasy about Yeats's rhetoric and about his own, Auden had famously declared, "For poetry makes nothing happen."

Yet in that section of the elegy, Auden used forms of the word "survive" three times. In their different ways, he and Yeats imagined poetry as a power opposing the worldly power of bankers, schoolmasters, and clergymen, or in Auden's case, Hitler. Mourning Yeats, Auden wrote:

> You were silly like us; your gift **survived** it all:
> The parish of rich women, physical decay,
> Yourself. Mad Ireland hurt you into poetry.
> Now Ireland has her madness and her weather still,
> For poetry makes nothing happen: it **survives**
> In the valley of its making where executives
> Would never want to tamper, flows on south
> From ranches of isolation and the busy griefs,
> Raw towns that we believe and die in; it **survives**,
> A way of happening, a mouth.

By the end of the poem, elegy has turned into a ringing declaration of the moral power of poetry:

> In the deserts of the heart
> Let the healing fountain start,
> In the prison of his days
> Teach the free man how to praise.

Poetry, in fact, is asked to do quite a lot. To be a happening, if not to "make something happen."

Every elegy for a poet acknowledges the death of the poet and strives for the survival of poetry. What is this survival? Why does it matter? These are questions Derek Walcott wrestled with all his life. He used that word, "survival," in his Nobel speech: "Survival is the triumph of stubbornness..." How is poetry not to be made "futile"? Let us pursue his question through one book, *Midsummer*.

Midsummer was published in 1984, roughly *nel mezzo del cammin* of the epic *cammin* of Walcott's writing life, counting from his *Twenty-Five Poems* in 1948. With *Midsummer*, he had behind him already a majestic body of work, including *The Gulf, Another Life, Sea Grapes, The Star-Apple Kingdom*, and *The Fortunate Traveller*—and I'm not even touching on the plays, which take up themes of political power far more directly than the poems do.

In *Another Life*, a single, book-length autobiographical poem from 1973, one feels lyric evolving toward epic. Into and around the story of the inspired, self-destructive painter Gregorias, an alter-ego for the aspiring poet, *Another Life* brings into full view the landscape of St. Lucia and its historical scars:

> Verandahs, where the pages of the sea
> are a book left open by an absent master

in the middle of another life—
I begin here again

the poem opens, and we are at once in Walcott-land, where
nature is seen as consubstantial with text—"the pages of
the sea/ are a book left open"— and a legacy of slavery
has to be read in that text—"by an absent master." Nor
can slavery, in the context of the Caribbean, be understood
as separate from the stories of the empires that jostled for
control of the islands, the Dutch, Spanish, the French, the
British. This, too, the poem sees:

as a sun, tired of empire, declined.

Another Life is the story of two St. Lucian artists, a
painter and a poet, struggling to envision their land and
its fate. They start from deprivation, colonial mongrels on
the outskirts of cultural and political power:

I had entered the house of literature as a houseboy,
filched as the slum child stole.

How should that slum child, just by seeing and singing,
assert, impose, another view, with so much authority
massed to crush him?

A few years later, that child has taken the shape of
Shabine, the sailor poet, rhapsode of "The Schooner Flight"
in the book *The Star-Apple Kingdom*:

I'm just a red nigger who love the sea,
I had a sound colonial education,
I have Dutch, nigger, and English in me,
and either I'm nobody, or I'm a nation.

Shabine fights colonial and post-colonial mythologies, all of which leave him out: "I met History once, and he ain't recognize me." In flight from wife and children, lover, political corruption and persecution, Shabine ships out on a schooner into the dream of the sea, where he has to defend his poetry with a knife when the cook, Vincie, steals his notebook and derides it in front of the crew. The knife flies into "the plump of his calf"; Shabine declares, "There wasn't much pain, just plenty blood, and Vincie and me best friend, / but none of them go fuck with my poetry again." If the life of poetry can sometimes feel like a knife fight, Shabine's best weapon isn't his blade, but his language: his glorious, hybrid, part-Elizabethan, part-Creole, ingeniously rhyming, rhythmical, and imagistic vernacular. And this is the weapon of Derek Walcott, who after all imagined Shabine and gave him voice:

> I shall scatter your lives like a handful of sand,
> I who have no weapon but poetry and
> The lances of palms and the sea's shining shield!

Midsummer appeared five years after *The Star-Apple Kingdom*. Walcott was fifty-four years old, and the tone is less ecstatic and triumphant than Shabine's. The middle-aged poet reconsiders, takes stock, and measures failure, making a new kind of poetry from those measures. The old Walcott themes survive in force—sea and land are embodied scripture, the wreckage of empire lies strewn around, the speaker is an alienated prodigal son at home nowhere. But these poems work out a new relation to language in a new relation to the private life—aging, friendship, love—and a new relation to the external powers. Because this is poetry, not philosophy, political science, or journalism, the relations are revealed not in theme or subject matter, but line by line, syllable by syllable, in alignment.

Midsummer acts like one long poem in fifty-four sections. It can be no accident that they tally the age of the poet when he wrote them. The poems don't resemble his earlier lyrics: the lines are consistently longer, varying between five and six beats; there are no stanza breaks; the poems sit like chunks of masonry on the page, and vaguely resemble sonnets, but sonnets that wanted more room, and took it. The tone is less high-pitched than before, verging on the conversational, and since the whole book is framed in affectionate addresses to Walcott's friend Joseph Brodsky, the tone is intimate, so the reader feels implicitly included in the friendship.

Let's begin with failure. The book opens with the poet-speaker in a jet carving down through the sky to land in Trinidad, another of his Antillean homes where he is not entirely at home. As in his Nobel lecture, he cites the Victorian historian James Anthony Froude, enthusiast of empire and author of *The English in the West Indies* of 1888. " 'No people there,' to quote Froude, 'in the true sense of the word,'" wrote Walcott in his speech. "No people. Fragments and echoes of real people, unoriginal and broken." Poem I of *Midsummer* sees those non-people in their non-culture through the "volumes of cloud" through which the jet bores down:

So a hole in their parchment opens, and suddenly, in a vast
dereliction of sunlight, there's that island known
to the traveller Trollope, and the fellow traveller Froude,
for making nothing. Not even a people...

Before we can even speak of the failure of poetry, we have to confront the idea of the failure of a whole culture, a people. The sequence of poems that follows rises to this challenge, to make real and visible what Froude couldn't and wouldn't see: a civilization rich in its hybrid languages, religions, suffering, and beauty. That defiant act of making starts right on the first page, as Walcott asks us to imagine "canefields set in stanzas" and nouns, like a crowd of egrets, skimming to find their branches "as simply as birds." This poetry is sacramental and incarnational: the landscape already has the shape of poems—canefields set in stanzas—and language acts in nature with the force of nature: those noun-egrets. But they need the poet to give them voice.

Walcott answers Froude with a show of force. Partly, imagistic force: metaphors teem and breed, the landscape ripples in a constant Ovidian proliferation. Partly, rhythmical force: the enjambing, loping lines pulse forward in long periodic sequences as "the trundling tires keep shaking and shaking the heart." And partly phonetic. The irregular rhymes perform their own little allegories. Their ingenuity echoes the fertility of the land; in rhymes as wild as those of Hopkins, the canefields "set in stanzas" rhyme with "a world that still stands as." In one of Walcott's favorite pairings—one he will take up again in the beautiful book *White Egrets* of 2010—"egrets" rhyme with "regrets." And look at the intelligence in spacing between rhyme words. Rhyme, to work expressively, must exploit the piquancy of difference in meaning played against similarity in sound. It matters keenly for Walcott's sense of Joseph Brodsky writing in Rome while he, Walcott, writes in Trinidad, that the words "Rome" and "home" should be separated by eleven lines: Rome is far from home, though they are linked. It matters even more that the last word of this first poem, "heart," which is also the last word of the whole book, should rhyme in the first poem with "apart," and that they should be separated by nineteen lines. In poem I, we must jump from "but pages in a damp culture that come apart," down to the last line for the rhyme: "the trundling tires keep shaking and shaking the heart." And the last two lines of the book: "Ah, Joseph, though no man ever dies in his own country, / the grateful grass will grow thick from his heart." The heart is apart, both for Brodsky, once a political prisoner, now expelled from his native Russia, and for Walcott, a wanderer and prodigal son of his beloved Antilles.

Midsummer starts with Froude's accusation of the failure of a colonized culture. Later poems in the book evoke other political powers before which poetry may seem to stand helpless. Mr. Kurtz, from Conrad's "Heart of Darkness," threatens poem IV: "Stay on the right bank in the imperial dream—/ the Thames, not the Congo." A cluster of poems—XXII, XXIII, XXIV—registers violence around the globe. XXII glances at the war tearing up Afghanistan and Russia, and in a widening panorama, "nation takes on nation, / and from their fury of pronunciation, / children lie torn on rubble for a noun." XXIII shows the Brixton race riots in England, and Walcott's own confronting of genteel English racism: "I was there to add some color to the British theater. / 'But the blacks can't do Shakespeare, they have no experience.' / This was true…" XXIV remembers the conquistadors penetrating the New World: "Was evil brought to this place/ with language?" this poem asks, in the mode of Caliban addressing Prospero. This is a poem more of questions than of answers, and it raises the deeper question with which we started; how can poetry survive the world's powers—imperialism, colonialism, genocide—and not come off as futile?

Shabine defended his poetry by throwing a knife and by chanting. The Walcott persona in *Midsummer* must do something harder. From considering the failure of a culture, he draws inward to consider personal failure: the failure of poems, and the failure of the aging body. Palinode is the engine here: radical self-correction en route, mid-stream. Poem III sets the scene in Port of Spain, Trinidad:

At the Queen's Park Hotel, with its white, high-ceilinged
    rooms,
I re-enter my first local mirror. A skidding roach
in the porcelain basin slides from its path to Parnassus.
Every word I have written took the wrong approach.
I cannot connect these lines with the lines in my face.

This passage chastens in every respect. The encounter
with the older self in the mirror leads to the grotesque
image of poet as skidding cockroach. Doubly humiliated:
the body aging, the face lined with the years; and the poet's
Parnassian delusions reprimanded in this stern reappraisal
in midlife: "Every word I have written took the wrong
approach." It's not clear what "the wrong approach" was;
all we know is that in midsummer, in midlife, the poet must
remake himself and remake his poetry. It was, perhaps,
too poetical before. Now it takes on a new, declarative
toughness. How, in the face of this perceived failure, can
the poem proceed; how can poetry proceed? Precisely from
this acknowledgment. It must start over; it must find a way
to connect its lines with the lines in the face, with painful
personal truth. For Walcott, in *Midsummer*, this will mean
a discipline of memory and observation, to give poetry "a
new approach," one that will not skid down the porcelain
basin. Poem III regathers its strength by returning to the
child within the man, his "small voice," early memory. Then
it turns to look around outside the hotel at the present, at
the taxis and racehorses and canefields, and gives itself
a shock of high voltage in the quotation from Traherne's
prose about the visionary power of childhood: "The corn
was orient and immortal wheat." Thus fortified, the poem
begins the book anew with a string of metaphors: "With
all summer to burn, / a breeze strolls down to the docks,
and the sea begins."

Midsummer unfolds in a complex drama of connecting inner to outer life. To redeem the Antilles from Froude, to redeem himself from the cockroach, the poet protagonist keeps a diary of sorts. We follow him through days in Trinidad, we follow him in displacements to Boston and England, we follow him back to childhood and forward again to the present. The poetry makes its case, line by line, by what it can make real to us. And it continually questions its own premises. Every step courts ethical and imaginative danger. Why should anyone care about a poet's making and unmaking his poems, that high solipsism? And how can we align the awareness of the world's injuries these poems record with the private alignments of memory and sensation they also describe?

Poetry is an art, largely, of alignment. Alignment: composition in lines rather than sentences, more than any other feature, distinguishes poetry from prose. Alignment also refers to political identification, especially of smaller powers with larger ones. In *Midsummer*, Walcott performs a set of alignments in all senses, lining up verses to acknowledge but at the same time to distance the coercive political alignments, to make imaginative room for freedom. The freedom that Shabine sought, shipping out on the Schooner Flight; the freedom Brodsky found, fleeing the gulag and the Soviet regime; the freedom Walcott imagines not just for himself, but for his people, his islands.

Poem VII of *Midsummer* starts, like so many of Walcott's poems, with observation:

> Our houses are one step from the gutter. Plastic curtains
> or cheap prints hide what is dark behind windows...

The description is visual, figurative, and interpretive. "One step from the gutter": the houses are near the street, spatially; in terms of advanced Western economies, they are poor, deprived, tasteless; with the word "gutter" we even brush up against a possible sense of moral depravity (a judgment the poem refuses). The description builds to a line that could be taken as Froudian indictment: "The hills have no echoes. Not the echo of ruins." That emptiness can also be read as a New World freedom from Old World corruptions, prejudice, ruins. And that Old World was a world, is still a world, of coercive imperial powers which mapped the globe according to their appetites, as poem VII sees in the cracked sidewalk in Port of Spain:

> Any crack in the sidewalk was made by the primal fault
> of the first map of the world, its boundaries and powers.

Poem VII, which started one step from the gutter, pulls the unspecified "you" back into childhood "whose vines fasten your foot," and then widens into a meditation on "all wanderers," asking us to think, simultaneously, of rootedness in a primal place and childhood, and of exile and uprootedness. The pronouns work hard here. We started with "Our houses": that seems to mean the houses of the Caribbean, belonging to a restricted "we." Not everybody's houses. Later, the poem contrasts a "you" and an "I" as it explores the opposition between political tyranny—Tomas Venclova, the poet kicked out of Soviet Lithuania, and Heberto Padilla tortured and deported by Castro's Cuba—and the private maps of freedom, exile, and a refusal of politics:

> or why should you suddenly think of Tomas Venclova,
> and why should I care about whatever they did to Herberto
> when exiles must make their own maps, when this asphalt
> takes you far from the action, past hedges of unaligned
>   flowers?

Let's look at those pronouns. Why does Walcott distinguish between a "you" and an "I" in thinking about the exiled poets: "why should you suddenly think of Tomas Venclova," "why should I care about whatever they did to Herberto"? The "you" might be specific and personal: since the whole book is somehow addressed to Brodsky, like Venclova an exile from the Soviet state, perhaps he's the one thinking of Venclova. But "you" also conventionally may include the reader, and just as conventionally sometimes projects an imagined version of the speaker. The "you" and the "I" here, thinking respectively of poets from the Soviet Union and the Caribbean, seem to partition the world's oppressions and at the same time to unite and generalize them. Out of that scenario, Poem VII in its final pun, declares its independence; declares poetry's freedom from the world's powers, in wielding poetry's own power, imagination and wordplay: "when exiles must make their own maps, when this asphalt/ takes you far from the action, past hedges of unaligned flowers?"

At least in the imagination, those unaligned flowers upend tyrants and governments. Poetry's lines remain politically unaligned in order to preserve their spiritual freedom. Yet they cannot claim innocence. Eden has been lost, in the Caribbean as elsewhere, and even in the almost pastoral world of childhood memory and picturesque jungle, the poem can't forget the political forces that shape life everywhere on the globe. To see the flowers as "unaligned" is to see them in terms of political systems that demand alignment. Poetry's lines nerve themselves, inevitably, against hostile powers.

Because of that opposition, and because of the capacious, flexible pronouns (I, you), Walcott's agon of the poet-at-work in *Midsummer* doesn't come across as solipsistic. It's a freedom most of us crave. It is to be shared. Poem IX carries the image of alignment from the political sphere to the personal. It dramatizes the poet's struggle to align nature and his "own nature," to align language and geography—which is his life work. Out of this record of effort and failure arises a vision of an idealized language, a goal glimpsed even as it recedes, thrumming with power even in its almost liturgical expression of frustration: too rapid, too patient, too frantic, too slow. Perhaps they never align ideally, nature and human nature. Poetry feels impossible and contradictory: too rapid, too patient…But impossibility is its medium. Metaphor and rhythm make their own reality, in this case an elemental reality of lightning, sea, wind, stone. In these lines, Walcott comes close to identifying human creative power with the Genesis power in nature, a power that outlasts empires. The poem almost seems to be written by lightning, the sea, the wind, and the stones rolled in the surf.

It touches earth, that branched diviner's rod
the lightning, like the swift note of a swallow on the staff
of four electric wires, while everything I read
or write goes on too long. Ah, to have
a tone colloquial and stiff,
the brevity of that short syllable, God,
all synthesis in one heraldic stroke,
like Li Po or a Chinese laundry mark! Walk
these hot streets, their signs a dusty backdrop stuck
to the maundering ego. The lines that jerk
into step do not fit any mold. More than time
keeps shifting. Language never fits geography
except when the earth and summer lightning rhyme.
When I was greener, I strained with a branch
to utter every tongue, language, and life at once.
More skillful now, I'm more dissatisfied.

They never align, nature and your
own nature. Too rapid the lightning's shorthand,
too patient the sea repeatedly tearing up paper,
too frantic the wind unraveling the same knot,
too slow the stones crawling toward language every night.

In "Tropic Zone," a longer sequence later in the book, Walcott once again ponders poetry and the powers. "Tropic Zone"'s eight poems are set in San Juan, Puerto Rico, in the Spanish-speaking Caribbean familiar but unfamiliar to the poet from the English and French Creole-speaking St. Lucia: "This is my ocean, but it is speaking/ another language." Politics are written into the most innocent appearances: the vines "drop like olive-green infantry/ over from Cuba"; "The wind is up early, campaigning/ with the leaflets of seagulls" (i). Yet into this predetermined colonial scene, the poet projects that old emptiness which could be either Froudian accusation or, conversely, the imaginative license for new creation: the creation of a new poem, a new culture:

The corners are empty. The boulevards open like novels
Waiting to be written. Clouds like the beginnings of stories.
(i)

"Tropic Zone" is excruciatingly aware of politics. "History will pierce you like a migraine," declares the poet-speaker in Poem ii. This history includes the extermination of the indigenous Indians by white colonists:

Blue skies convert all genocide into fiction.

The speaker's migraine is brought on not just by the contemplation of the original sins of colonial conquest, but by their aftermath, the bitter knowledge that revolutionary utopias have brought on their own horrors, like the grim scene in Poem vii where "a new ogre/ erects his bronzes over the parks." The drastic struggles have been reduced to kitsch, capitalist and socialist, like the "nationalized Eden" in the murals of the hotel and the beer ads, in Poem iii, or the gringo-bandidos movies in Poem iv; the poet-protagonist seems as ironically detached from all political solutions as the old men in white suits muttering in Poem v, avoiding bicycles: "Their revolution is that all things come in circles." So that, "For each old man, in his white panama hat,/ there is no ideology in the light."

Where does that leave poetry? The history-migraine in "Tropic Zone" threatens poetry with futility, and the poet with cynicism and paralysis. In facing this impasse Walcott seizes his opportunity. Resisting the power of bankers, schoolmasters, and clergymen, as of conquistadors, tyrants, and tourist moguls, the poet refuses "alignment" and creates his own revolution in lines that refuse the "linear time" of historical determinism:

> but a man, drawn to the seawall, crouches like a question,
> or a prayer, and my own prayer is to write
> lines as mindless as the ocean's of linear time,
> since time is the first province of Caesar's jurisdiction. (ii)

It's important to note the distinction being made here. Walcott is not claiming to be a holy fool, "mindless" of history. The poems are, on the contrary, painfully mindful, mindful of the natural surroundings and of historical and political force. Hence the migraine. They are mindless of linear time: mindless of, deliberately resistant to, any imperial, historicist account that would impose its own justification of power. That would be Caesar's jurisdiction. In opposing colonialism and its political aftermath,

Walcott's "Tropics" are the opposite of escapist. These poems are not on vacation in a moral void. But they pit their lines against forced alignment, and they set poetry's cadences, the rhythmical time of patterned memory and meaning, against rigid linear time and its murderous political logic.

Auden concluded his elegy for Yeats with a prayer and a statement of faith in the power of poetry to heal, even in the teeth—especially in the teeth—of disaster:

> In the desert of the heart
> Let the healing fountain start,
> In the prison of his days
> Teach the free man how to praise.

Derek Walcott concluded *Midsummer* with a similar, if less grandiloquent turn. If poetry is to assume its own powers, it is by making the real *real* to us, freeing it from abstractions, clichés, and mind-deadening policy blather. That reality, in rhythm and image, outlives empires. A recent poem in *White Egrets* begins: "And then there was no Empire all of a sudden." Poetry's is a Genesis power, freed from religious doctrine but retaining sacred creative energy and fueled by love. Love of country, love of friend, love of language. The Word in these lines is capitalized; it's the word made flesh in Walcott's secular mythology, a power that trumps politics. Here is how Derek Walcott teaches the free man—let us say, the free person—how to praise:

> Where's my child's hymnbook, the poems edged in gold leaf,
> the heaven I worship with no faith in heaven,
> as the Word turned toward poetry in its grief?
> Ah, bread of life, that only love can leaven!
> Ah, Joseph, though no man ever dies in his own country,
> the grateful grass will grow thick from his heart.

CONTRIBUTORS

Peter Balakian's books include *Ozone Journal*, winner of the Pulitzer Prize, *Black Dog of Fate* winner of the PEN/ Albrand Award, and his new book of poems *No Sign* published by The University of Chicago Press. He teaches at Colgate University.

Robert Bensen's latest book is *What Lightning Spoke: New and Selected Poems* (Bright Hill Press, 2022). He is emeritus Professor of English and Director of Writing at Hartwick College, where he taught from 1978-2017.

Sven Birkerts is co-editor of *AGNI* and former director of the Bennington Writing Seminars. His most recent book is *Speak, Memory* in the Ig Books Bookmarked series, a meditation on Nabokov's memoir and the works of time. He used to audit Walcott's seminar at BU and took much from that incantatory instruction.

Peter Campion is the author most recently of *One Summer Evening at the Falls*. A recipient of the Guggenheim Fellowship and the Joseph Brodsky Rome Prize, he teaches in the Department of English and MFA writing program at the University of Minnesota.

Rachel DeWoskin is the award-winning author of five novels: *Someday We Will Fly; Banshee; Blind; Big Girl Small; Repeat After Me;* the memoir *Foreign Babes in Beijing;* and the poetry collection, *Two Menus*. Her essays and poems have appeared in publications including *The New Yorker, Vanity Fair, Ploughshares,* and *New Voices* from the Academy of American Poets. She is on the fiction faculty at the University of Chicago, and affiliated faculty in Jewish and East Asian Studies.

Zayd Ayers Dohrn is a playwright and screenwriter. His work includes *Mother Country Radicals* (Tribeca Official Selection), *The Profane* (Horton Foote New American Play Prize), *Sick* (Theatre Masters Visionary Playwrights Award), and *Permanent Whole Life* (IRNE Award for Best New Play at Boston Playwrights' Theatre). He is a Professor at Northwestern University and Director of the MFA in Writing for Screen + Stage.

Martin Edmunds' poems have appeared in *Agni, The New Yorker, The Paris Review, A Public Space, Little Star, The Nation*, and *Consequence*, and are featured on *Poetry Daily, Vox Populi*, and the Yeats Society of NY website. His new book, *Flame in a Stable*, and his chapbook *Black Ops* were published by Arrowsmith Press; Donald Hall chose his first book, *The High Road to Taos*, for the National Poetry Series. He co-wrote the screenplay for the film *Passion in the Desert* (Roland Films/Fine Line Features), an adaptation of the Balzac story.

Thomas Sayers Ellis is the author of *The Maverick Room, Skin Inc.: Identity Repair Poems, Crank Shaped Notes* and *Mexico*, a book of photographs. He is the co-founder of *Heroes Are Gang Leaders*, a free jazz literary ensemble of artists and musicians who were awarded the American Book Award for Oral Literature. In 2015, Ellis received a Guggenheim Fellowship for poetry.

Carolyn Forché is a poet, memoirist, and translator. She is the author of the memoir *What You Have Heard Is True: A Memoir of Witness and Resistance* (Penguin Press, 2019), which was a finalist for the National Book Award, and five books of poetry. Her most recent poetry book, *In the*

Lateness of the World (Penguin, 2020) was a finalist for the Pulitzer Prize. She is also editor of *Against Forgetting: Twentieth Century Poetry of Witness* (W.W. Norton, 1993) and co-editor of *Poetry of Witness: The Tradition in English 1500-2001*, with Duncan Wu (W.W. Norton, 2014). She has translated five books of poetry, most recently *America* by Fernando Valverde (Copper Canyon Press, 2021). She is University Professor at Georgetown University, and lives in Maryland with her husband, Harry Mattison.

Jonathan Galassi is Chairman and Executive Editor of Farrar, Straus & Giroux and worked with Derek Walcott from the late 1980s until his death.

Dan Hunter is an award-winning playwright, songwriter, teacher, founding partner of Hunter Higgs, LLC, and inventor of H-IQ. He served as managing director of the Boston Playwrights Theatre, published numerous plays with Baker's Plays, and has performed topical humor in song on ABC, NPR, BBC and CNN. Formerly executive director of the Massachusetts Advocates for the Arts, Sciences, and Humanities, he also served as Director of the Iowa Department of Cultural Affairs. His forthcoming book, *Atrophy, Apathy & Ambition*, offers a layman's investigation into artificial intelligence. He is the author of several books of humor, including *Let's Keep Des Moines a Private Joke, Iowa?...It's a State, and his most recent Pandemic Panacea: Laughing through Quarantine.*

Kirun Kapur is the author of three books of poetry, *Women in the Waiting Room* (Black Lawrence Press, 2020), a finalist for the National Poetry Series, the Julie Suk Award and the Massachusetts Book Award; *Visiting Indira Gandhi's*

Palmist (Elixir Press, 2015) which won the Arts & Letters Rumi Prize and the Antivenom Poetry Award; and the chapbook *All the Rivers in Paradise* (UChicago Arts, 2022). She serves as editor at the *Beloit Poetry Journal* and teaches at Amherst College, where she is director of the Creative Writing Program.

Karl Kirchwey's eighth book of poems *Good Apothecary* is forthcoming from Northwestern University Press, and his anthology *Poems of Healing* appeared in the Everyman's Library Pocket Poets series in 2021. He teaches in the MFA Program in Creative Writing at Boston University.

Adam Kirsch is a poet and critic whose books include "The Discarded Life: Poems" and "The Modern Element: Essays on Contemporary Poetry."

John Robert Lee is a Saint Lucian writer. His *Pierrot* (2020) and *Collected Poems 1975-2015* (2017) are published by Peepal Tree Press. His *Saint Lucian Writers and Writing: an Index of Published Works* (2019) is issued by Papillote Press.

Glyn Maxwell is a poet, playwright and librettist. His latest book of poems is *How The Hell Are You* (Picador) which was shortlisted for the T S Eliot Prize. He wrote the popular critical guidebook *On Poetry* (Oberon), and is currently writing a new English libretto for Wagner's *The Flying Dutchman* for Opera UpClose. He is head of studies and teaches at The Poetry School

Askold Melnyczuk's most recent book, *The Man Who Would Not Bow* (stories), appeared in 2021. He has published four novels as well as poems, essays, stories, translations and reviews in the *TLS, New England Review, The New York Times, Poetry, APR, The Los Angeles Times*, etc. He is founding editor of *Agni* and Arrowsmith Press.

Caryl Phillips was born in St Kitts, grew up in Britain, and now lives in the United States. He is the author of numerous works of fiction and nonfiction.

Steven Ratiner, Arlington's Poet Laureate, has published three poetry chapbooks, and is completing work on three full-length collections. His work has appeared in scores of journals in America and abroad including *Parnassus, Agni, Hanging Loose, Poet Lore, Salamander, QRLS* (Singapore), *HaMusach* (Israel), and *Poetry Australia* – and he's also written poetry criticism for *The Christian Science Monitor, The San Francisco Chronicle, Arrowsmith Journal*, and *The Washington Post. Giving Their Word – Conversations with Contemporary Poets* was re-issued in a paperback edition (University of Massachusetts Press) and features interviews with many of poetry's most important figures. His weekly *Red Letter Poems* feature poets from across New England and beyond.

Eva Salzman is a dual citizen of the USA and UK. Her books include *Double Crossing: New & Selected Poems* and *Women's Work: Modern Women Poets Writing in English*. Christine Tobin and Gary Carpenter have set her lyrics/libretti. Her publications include *New Yorker, Kenyon Review, TLS, Dark Horse*, and *the Guardian* and Independent newspapers. A project on the late poet Sarah Hannah is in the works.

Bob Scanlan is Artistic Director of the Poets' Theatre. He was Professor of the Practice of Theatre and Chair of the

Committee on Dramatics at Harvard University, Literary Director of the American Repertory Theatre, and Director of Drama at MIT.

Tom Sleigh is the author of eleven books of poetry, including *The King's Touch*, just out from Graywolf Press, as well as *House of Fact, House of Ruin, Station Zed,* and *Army Cats*. His most recent book of essays, *The Land Between Two Rivers: Writing In an Age of Refugees*, recounts his time as a journalist in the Middle East and Africa. He has been a Kingsley Tufts Award winner, a Guggenheim Fellow, A Lila Wallace Award recipient, as well as having received the John Updike Award and an Individual Writer Award from the American Academy of Arts and Letters, and two NEA grants in poetry. His poems appear in *The New Yorker, The Atlantic, Threepenny Review, Poetry, The Southern Review, Harvard Review, Raritan, The Common* and many other magazines. He is a Distinguished Professor in the MFA Program at Hunter College.

Kate Snodgrass is the Artistic Director of Derek Walcott's Boston Playwrights' Theatre and Co-Founder of the Elliot Norton Award-winning Boston Theater Marathon, now in its 25th year. She directs the MFA Program in Playwriting at Boston University and is a former National Chair of Playwriting with the Kennedy Center American College Theater Festival. A StageSource 2001 "Theatre Hero," Kate was awarded Boston's Theatre Critics' Elliot Norton Award for Sustained Excellence in 2012. Her Heideman Award-winning play *Haiku* has been widely anthologized, and her radio play *Overture* can be heard on the Huntington Theatre website in "Dream Boston." Her full-length play *The Art of Burning* will premiere at the Huntington Theatre Company and Hartford Stage in January-March, 2023.

Jacob Strautmann's book of poems *The Land of the Dead Is Open for Business* is available from Four Way Books. Awarded a 2018 Massachusetts Poetry Fellowship by the Massachusetts Cultural Council, Jacob Strautmann's poems have appeared in *The Boston Globe, The Appalachian Journal, Southern Humanities Review* and *Blackbird*.

Rosanna Warren teaches in the Committee on Social Thought at the University of Chicago. Her most recent books are *So Forth*, a collection of poems, and *Max Jacob: A Life in Art and Letters*, a biography, both from W.W. Norton in 2020.

Acknowledgments

Special Thanks to the Walcott family, to his daughters Anna and Lizzie, for their support of this project and for permission to reproduce the painting gracing the cover of this book.

I would like to thank Ezra Fox, Lara Stecewycz, and Gerard Robertson for their assistance in preparing this volume. My gratitude to Victoria Fox and Jonathan Galassi of Farrar, Straus and Giroux for permission to quote from Derek Walcott's published and unpublished work. Thanks too to all the contributors for taking the time to re-immerse in Walcott's work and for meeting our deadlines. And thanks again to Ezra Fox for his inventive design solutions: grace under the pressure is how Hemingway defined courage, and of that Ezra has an abundance.

For me the chance to sink back into Derek's poetry has been a joyful and buoying task. I only hope this volume brings new readers to a rediscovery of Walcott's magnificent work.

Askold Melnyczuk
Medford, May 2022

Books by
ARROWSMITH PRESS

Girls by Oksana Zabuzhko

Bula Matari/Smasher of Rocks by Tom Sleigh

This Carrying Life by Maureen McLane

Cries of Animal Dying by Lawrence Ferlinghetti

Animals in Wartime by Matiop Wal

Divided Mind by George Scialabba

The Jinn by Amira El-Zein

Bergstein
edited by Askold Melnyczuk

Arrow Breaking Apart by Jason Shinder

Beyond Alchemy by Daniel Berrigan

Conscience, Consequence: Reflections on Father Daniel Berrigan
edited by Askold Melnyczuk

Ric's Progress by Donald Hall

Return To The Sea by Etnairis Rivera

The Kingdom of His Will by Catherine Parnell

Eight Notes from the Blue Angel by Marjana Savka

Fifty-Two by Melissa Green

Music In—And On—The Air by Lloyd Schwartz

Magpiety by Melissa Green

Reality Hunger by William Pierce

Soundings: On The Poetry of Melissa Green
edited by Sumita Chakraborty

The Corny Toys by Thomas Sayers Ellis

Black Ops by Martin Edmunds

Museum of Silence by Romeo Oriogun

City of Water by Mitch Manning

Passeggiate by Judith Baumel

Persephone Blues by Oksana Lutsyshyna

The Uncollected Delmore Schwartz
edited by Ben Mazer

The Light Outside by George Kovach

The Blood of San Gennaro by Scott Harney
edited by Megan Marshall

No Sign by Peter Balakian

Firebird by Kythe Heller

The Selected Poems of Oksana Zabuzhko
edited by Askold Melnyczuk

The Age of Waiting by Douglas J. Penick

Manimal Woe by Fanny Howe

Crank Shaped Notes by Thomas Sayers Ellis

The Land of Mild Light by Rafael Cadenas
edited by Nidia Hernández

The Silence of Your Name by Alexandra Marshall

Flame in a Stable by Martin Edmunds

Mrs. Schmetterling by Robin Davidson

This Costly Season by John Okrent

Thorny by Judith Baumel

The Invisible Borders of Time: Five Female Latin American Poets
edited by Nidia Hernández

Some of You Will Know by David Rivard

The Forbidden Door: The Selected Poetry of Lasse Söderberg
translated by Lars Gustaf Andersson & Carolyn Forché

Unrevolutionary Times by Houman Harouni

ARROWSMITH is named after the late William Arrowsmith, a renowned classics scholar, literary and film critic. General editor of thirty-three volumes of *The Greek Tragedy in New Translations*, he was also a brilliant translator of Eugenio Montale, Cesare Pavese, and others. Arrowsmith, who taught for years in Boston University's University Professors Program, championed not only the classics and the finest in contemporary literature, he was also passionate about the importance of recognizing the translator's role in bringing the original work to life in a new language.

*Like the arrowsmith who turns his arrows straight and true,
a wise person makes his character straight and true.*

— Buddha

CPSIA information can be obtained
at www.ICGtesting.com
Printed in the USA
LVHW101443110822
725656LV00002B/68